LACE of LOVE®

Inspiring stories of
New Shoes
for Needy Kids

by Jeanne Nara Nealon

LACES of LOVE®

www.lacesoflove.org

This is a collection of personal stories from those whose lives have been touched by Laces of Love Charitable Foundation, Inc.

Jeanne Nara Nealon
Co-founder, Laces of Love®

Ubi-Caritas-est-vera-Deus-ibi-est

"Where True Charity and Love Dwell,
God himself is there."
~ Servant Song

Dedication

This book honors the children who have stuffed the toes of their shoes with tissue paper to make them fit, used cardboard as insoles to keep their feet dry, or slogged to school in Dad's huge old shoes because they had nothing else to wear. We honor the girl who came to school with blistered feet from pinchy shoes and for the high school student who wore slippers because that's all she had. This book celebrates the many children who smiled and cried when they received a new pair of shoes and the supporters who provided them.

We at Laces of Love® believe that no child should go barefoot in our schools. These are their stories, painful but true, and the intolerable situations they've endured.

The purchase of this book and your donations will help provide new shoes for a needy child.

Thank you!

We can do no great things, only small things with great love.
~*St. Teresa of Calcutta*
(Mother Teresa)

Table of Contents

Early "Laces" 1
Background: The Shoestrings 1
Connecting "Laces" One Step at a Time 5
Who are these Children? 9
Top Dog.. 11
The Happiest Day of My Life..................... 21
Prince 23
Crowded Quarters 26
Tamika's Noisy Shoes........................... 30
My Brand New Feet 33
Skipping 35
Run Away Soles 37
It's Your Lucky Day 39
The Morning Walkers........................... 43
The Dance 47
Do You Have Glue?............................. 48
Tyson's Shoe Tags............................. 50
High Tops For Tender Foot..................... 53
Right on Target................................ 55
We Have the Same Name? 57
Goody Two Shoes.............................. 60
Walk in Her Shoes 64
Slipping By 67
The Real Deal 71
Sole Sistas 74
Shoes for Sale 82
Eli and Two Different Shoes 91
Footwork 93
Letters of Love 97
Call to Action (How to Help) 103
A Note from the Author 115
Source List for Quotations..................117
About the Author 119

Early "Laces"

Early in my teaching career, I drove a student home after a school performance. I didn't know he lived in a migrant camp with multiple family members in a very small space. It was in this moment I realized that because the family was poor, he and his siblings took turns sharing the few shoes that they owned. This experience changed my life.

Background: The Shoestrings

Growing up in a family with eight children, co-founder, Jeanne Nara Nealon, learned from her parents that the true meaning of love is in giving. When she was a little girl, her mom gave her a book, *The Giving Tree* by Shel Silverstein. From this book—and parents who lived the true meaning of love by reaching out and giving to others in spiritual, emotional, or physical need—she formed her commitment to follow the same path.

Jeanne and her sister, Mary Myrmo, watched a film called *Children from Heaven* about two children who shared one pair of shoes because they were so poor. After driving her student home, the realization of children sharing shoes in her **own** community was shocking. "In **my own** community?" played like a mantra on the drive home.

After her experience at a migrant camp and realizing children were actually sharing shoes, the sisters took action. They started to collect new tennis shoes and deliver them to needy children at local schools. When Jeanne was asked to give a motivational speech, she requested that one pair of new shoes be donated in lieu of payment. One of the first groups to collect shoes was the Boy Scouts. It was a memorable moment when she walked in and found all fifteen, smiling boys *each* holding a new pair of shoes.

After speaking to a group of teachers one morning, a wonderful woman named Susy Warren approached her. "Jeanne, I want to help with your organization and mission to provide needy children with new shoes." She found that Susy had experience and knowledge in non-profit organizations and philanthropic giving. What a gift she was! Susy became a mentor, a volunteer executive director, a friend, and she was instrumental in helping create Laces of Love® as a charitable organization.

Today, Laces of Love encourages bonds between kind, generous people and children in the community who are facing challenges. As a result of speaking engagements, shoe drives, shoe parties, and donations, the all-volunteer Board of Directors along with countless supporters and volunteers have provided over 100,000 Laces of Love shoes to needy children of Collier and Lee counties in Southwest Florida. The number continues to grow each school year, along with the needs of children in these communities.

The name Laces of Love® is a registered Service Mark. It may not be used by any individual or organization without the expressed, written approval of the Laces of Love® Board of Directors.

The three co-founders of Laces of Love®, from left to right:
Mary Nara Myrmo, Jeanne Nara Nealon, Susan Warren

Mission Statement:

The mission of Laces of Love® is to provide NEW shoes to low
income and disadvantaged children in Collier and Lee counties,
Florida. Shoes are distributed through the schools and through
other non-profits that serve "Laces" kids.

Where there is great love, there are always miracles.

~Willa Cather

We have been able to meet some wonderful families from Immokalee through Laces of Love. Jeanne (middle right) with her husband and son and Undreas Harrison (middle left), with her sons. The families continue to be very close friends since meeting in 2006. Pictured left to right: T'Shumbi Johnson, Don Nealon, Undreas Harrison, Jeanne, Bryce Nealon, and D'Ernest Johnson.

Let us carry Mother Teresa's smile in our hearts and give
it to those whom we meet along our journey.
~Pope Francis

Connecting "Laces" One Step at a Time

The Laces of Love Charitable Foundation, Inc. is a 501-c-3 not-for-profit organization that provides shoes to low-income, disadvantaged children, and children in crisis. It also educates the public about the needs of these children. Since its incorporation in 2005, Laces of Love® has provided over 100,000 pairs of new shoes to needy students in South Florida.

One person or a group can donate new shoes and create a joyful difference in a child's life. Many educators, nurses, administrators, and counselors have witnessed the transformation when a child takes off his worn-out, holey shoes—some without soles—and puts on new shoes. The realization that someone cared enough to give her new shoes when her old taped-up, glued-together shoes were painful to wear can change a child's life. Suddenly, an act of generosity chases away the embarrassment and pain. There's a moment of pure gratitude and disbelief when an athlete receives the right shoes for his or her sport. Imagine...a new pair of shoes...an item many of us take for granted.

Laces of Love is simply about providing a pair of shoes to a needy child. Giving a new pair of shoes to a child is a very special and personal moment, but many guidance counselors, teachers, school nurses and principals have sent us emails, letters and stories about their observations. From the generosity of others to a needy child, the connection is inspiring and it's important to share these stories with the many supporters who have graciously contributed to Laces of Love.

This small book is written with love to enlighten you to the needs of children in our community and in other communities. For storytelling purposes and for simplicity, some stories have been combined and the names of the students have been changed. The stories are real; they are heart-wrenching, full of sadness, and distress, yet they are also full of JOY.

The very first pair of shoes I gave to a child in my classroom (the boy from the migrant camp) became the beginning of an incredible journey that transformed into Laces of Love. I hope you'll join the journey.

Jeanne Nara Nealon, President/Co-founder
Laces of Love Charitable Foundation, Inc.

Jeanne giving shoes at an outreach event.

"Sometimes," said Pooh, "the smallest things
take up the most room in your heart."

~A.A. Milne, from
Winnie-the-Pooh

A thank you card sent to Laces of Love from
a local elementary school.

Nelia Perez receiving a much needed new pair of shoes
at New Horizons After School Super Kids Club.

And good neighbors make a huge
difference in the quality of life. I agree.

~*Robert Fulghum*

Who Are these Children?

When I speak to the community, I'm asked, "Jeanne, who are these children that need shoes? Where do they live?"

I simply tell them, "In our own backyards."

It's heart-breaking to see the number of under-privileged families who have settled in Collier and Lee counties who live and labor for a pittance. Some are migrant workers who move with the harvesting seasons. Some are middle-class families that have fallen into hard times during hard years. They are good-hearted, caring people who are so willing to work they accept any menial jobs they can find to provide for their families.

This letter is like many we receive every month. It's from a struggling mom who lost her husband last year. She works two jobs and is simply trying to make ends meet.

Dear Laces of Love,

I'm so grateful for your help. I have two children and never thought I'd need this support. My husband passed away suddenly and I have been struggling financially to put food on the table and pay medical bills.

When school started, I only had enough extra money to buy one pair of new shoes for one of my two children. When my sons went to bed, I looked over my monthly bills and pulled out my checkbook. Suddenly, there was a tap on my door.

My oldest son came into my room and said that he could wear last year's school shoes and to buy his younger brother the new shoes. He was starting high school and I knew his old shoes were too tight, the shoes were ripped and his toes pushed through the top of the old shoes. When he left my room that night, I cried. Yet, he had said, "Mom, buy my younger brother new shoes for school."

I couldn't believe it when the school nurse at the high school called me and asked if she could give my oldest son a new pair of shoes from Laces of Love. It was an answer to a prayer.

Thank you Laces of Love, you've given my children new shoes and you have given me hope.

Love and Blessings,
A very grateful mom

Top Dog

Marching into the classroom that very first day with excitement igniting my smile, I wanted to jump on the desk and shout, "This is my very first day of teaching! You have no idea how excited I am to teach you English!" Instead, I opened the attendance log, smiled carefully and gazed out at 32 pair of eyes staring at me in Room 7. I pronounced almost every name incorrectly that first day, fumbling through six classes of chattering adolescents. For most first-year teachers, this could make them shiver, but I was quirky enough to know exactly who I was spending time with this year. Each class raced down the halls and stumbled into their seats in Room 7, teasing, carousing and demonstrating unusual antics and behaviors notorious for middle school. However, it was Sal, the tall young man with a grin that stood out in my last period class.

Strutting into my classroom, nodding and greeting everyone present, Sal's physical condition matched his outgoing personality. He liked to draw attention to himself by flexing his biceps under his tight-fitting shirt.

"So Miss, you look kinda young to be teachin'. How old are you exactly?"

Surprised by his bold approach, I hesitated as I pulled a desk toward him to sit down. He grinned, plopped down into the chair and said, "This is gonna be fun, prob'ly my favorite class this year."

"Great, let's get started," I replied as I searched for his name on my class roster.

The rest of the class filed in with high fives to Sal as they passed his seat.

"Hey Bud!" they'd say and fist-bump his hand.

"Wuzzup, Sal?"

"Whoa, you're in my class? All right, big man."

"Lookin' good, Big Guy."

"Sal, hey dude!"

Each student had a connection with this popular kid with the gigantic smile. As the weeks passed, Sal showed more of himself, constantly stretching and flexing his big muscles in class. With each move, the girls would "Ooohhh" and "Ahhhhhh" at Sal's displays. He was excellent at building muscles, but not building his school studies. He lacked the grades, I discovered, because he was barely doing enough to get by in each of his classes.

I started the school year off with my favorite childhood story, *The Giving Tree* by Shel Silverstein. I explained to my students about being "giving trees" to others. I remember that first year as the eighth graders would dash out of my room on a Friday afternoon while I reminded them to be giving trees to their parents.

"We know, Miss, be a giving tree," they would shout loud and clear and giggle all the way down the hall.

After class one day, I stopped Sal and asked, "Sal, what do you want to be when you grow up? What do you want to do with your life?"

He grinned and avoided my question, so I asked again. "Really, Sal, what do you want to do with your life?"

Sal looked a little uncomfortable. "I don't know, Miss. I guess I will follow in my dad's footsteps and older brother's, since I wear his old shoes." He pulled his backpack over his shoulder, turned and said, "Have a nice weekend, Miss, and don't forget," he flashed a grin, "be a giving tree!"

For the first time, I noticed the old shoes that were on his feet, as he awkwardly left my classroom that day. I wanted Sal to work harder and make good grades, but he had a flip attitude about schoolwork and setting higher goals for himself at school. He was clearly one of the smartest students in my class and yet turned in average work.

As the Drama Coach, I spent long hours on drama practice and play rehearsals during the first months of school. I cast every student that showed up for the "Charlie Brown's Christmas" try-outs, except for the part of Snoopy. After all, Snoopy didn't have any lines, he was a big dog and couldn't talk. I planned on just putting a cut-out poster board of Snoopy on the side of the stage for the performance, that is, until our home-economics teacher approached me one afternoon.

I could tell from Miss Ria's voice she had special news for me on this particular day after drama practice. "Shhhh, follow me," she said with a finger to her lips and motioning down the hall with the other.

When we entered her Home Ec room, she pointed to the cabinet. There, hanging in fuzzy white, faux fur was a magnificent Snoopy costume with big black spots sewn perfectly all over the soft material and a paper mâché head sitting on her front desk.

I gasped. "Oh my gosh, Miss Ria, it's the most beautiful costume I've ever seen." I was gasping for two reasons: one, I hadn't cast the part of Snoopy; and two, because the paper mâché head was very large—and I assumed heavy—as it sat so firmly on the desk. While I pondered that someone playing the part of Snoopy needed to be strong, I glanced over at Miss Ria.

"Isn't it wonderful? My class worked so hard on the paper mâché head." Touching the head and admiring their work, she continued to explain, "And we designed the costume together as a class project! I can't wait to see who you cast in the part of Snoopy."

As I lifted the head and its weight, I suddenly realized how to resolve this problem. The student who played the part of Snoopy needed to a large and strong person. Possibly a body-builder? I thought.

The next day I spoke to Sal and encouraged him to play the part of Snoopy.

"What do I gotta do, Miss?" he asked with a puzzled look on his face.

"Sal," I breeched the subject lightly, "you don't have to memorize any lines, because Snoopy doesn't talk. You just have to wear the costume and walk onto the stage." I did my best to reassure him.

"No lines to memorize?" he asked.

"No lines at all," I said. "The costume is wonderful, but the head is really heavy. I need someone who is big, strong, and can carry the Snoopy head on his shoulders." I looked at him hopefully.

"Hmmm," Sal thought out loud while flexing his muscles. "I am the strongest kid in the eighth grade and everybody knows it."

I nodded. "You're strong all right. So, will you please play the part of Snoopy?"

He looked at me and then said, "I'll do it on one condition."

"Whatever you need. What's your condition?"

"I want to be antonym." He flashed me a pleased smile as he waited for my response.

"What?" I asked.

"Antonym. I want to stay an antonym. I don't want anyone to know it's me under the paper mâché head—until I show myself." His voice was confident and strong.

"Oh!" I said. "You want to remain anonymous." I was careful in correcting him. If he had just listened in my class, I thought.

"Well, can I remain anonymous?" Sal asked proudly, saying the word correctly this time.

I looked at him and smiled. "Sure, no one will know who's under that Snoopy head until you take it off."

Thrilled with the deal he'd made, Sal reached over and tried on the head. It fit perfectly.

In the days to follow, the excitement for the play was building and I realized that Sal was working harder in class. His recent assignments were all completed and he earned 100 percent on his grammar test. He had accepted the role of Snoopy, but he had also decided to try hard in the classroom and be a strong student academically. I directed several positive comments to Sal and reinforced his efforts to work harder in English.

As the night of the performance arrived, I was making last minute preparations with lighting and microphones. Sal was situated in an off-stage, secluded area to wait for the surprise entrance.

Unaware of the magical impact that was about to happen, I was frantically motioning Sal to come out of the hidden area stage right. He was playing with the small tail attached to the back of the costume and he looked magnificent. With great anticipation, I shuffled him onto the stage during the song.

The very moment Sal walked onto the stage, he became the Snoopy everyone knew and loved. He wiggled his backside; he played with his tail and flipped his droopy ears. He was very animated as he flopped down by the other cast members begging for a pat of approval and love. The cast reacted to Snoopy with enthusiasm and he became the character to watch.

Sal was enjoying the captive audience as he started to show off and dance a one-of-a-kind dance. The audience cheered, laughed, and then something magical happened. Suddenly, Sal began his usual fit-body routine. In the Snoopy costume, he flexed his muscles, did deep knee bends, jogged around the stage, and oozed enthusiasm. Within moments, the audience began chanting, "Sal, Sal, Sal," clapping and cheering.

The entire cast started to clap on stage and chant as well. "Sal, Sal, Sal!"

Behind stage, my heart started pounding and I realized, They know!

As cast members ran onto the stage for the final song, Sal lifted the paper mâché head from his shoulders and the audience jumped to their feet in a standing ovation. The cast cheered as Sal proudly lifted the head of the costume over his head like a champion fighter after the title was announced.

"Sal, Sal, Sal!" the audience continued to cheer wildly.

We had worked for six weeks straight on the play and Sal showed up for two rehearsals and stole the show! He was truly the champion that night; the "Top Dog" we later called him.

The second performance ended late on Saturday night and an hour later I was loading costumes and boxes of props into my 1981 hatchback. As I carried the last box to the car, I noticed someone familiar seated under the school flagpole. There, beneath the light, was the large Snoopy head with Sal next to it.

Confused, I asked, "Sal, why are you still here?"

He looked up and paused for a moment. "Hey, Miss, well, you see…" he stumbled over his words. "Well, Miss, um…"

"Sal," I asked, "what's going on? Why are you here? The show ended two hours ago. It's really late."

"Well, my family came to the performance Friday night and tonight I have to wait for my dad and uncles to pick me up in the truck. They're going to be late coming from the fields. My family are migrant workers and work two or three farms a day. They pick until they're done or it's too dark. I have to wait for the truck."

I offered Sal a ride home. He shook his head several times.

"Sal, look, you can ride with me. I'll take you home." I pleaded with Sal until I convinced him to get in the car. We both were completely covered in mosquito bites by then.

As we ventured down the dirt roads, I realized Sal had never talked about his family in class. He was wearing his old shoes and a torn shirt.

The star of the play seemed quiet and nervous. He started tapping his foot anxiously, slumped down in his seat, and pouted. We drove down back roads that I didn't even know existed. We drove for about twenty minutes when Sal shouted, "Stop, Miss! Let me out right here." His voice was firm and he insisted that I stop the car.

"No," I told him sternly. "I'm not letting you out of the car in the middle of nowhere. It's dark and I'm taking you to your house. Tell me which way to go."

He looked at me with a sadness I had never seen before.

"Sal," I said, "tell me where you live."

He looked at me, then he sighed and looked down.

"Please, it's okay." I was concerned about this troubled young man who sat in my passenger seat.

Sal looked at me, then looked out the windshield at the long dirt road. He stared for what seemed like a very long time. Then he pointed to the next road. "Turn right. I live down there."

Turning down the next dirt road, I imagined the newspapers the next day. I shared my wild imagination with Sal hoping to create a giggle.

"Sal, newspaper headlines tomorrow will be: Teacher, Student and Car Eaten by Alligators!"

"*Si*, Miss! *Si, el caiman!*"

We both laughed as my car went over one mound of dirt, a little farther, and then another mound of dirt. It was dark and damp. I heard pebbles and stones hitting against the fender as I drove over yet another mound of dirt, and finally, I saw lights in the distance.

An old beat up trailer was situated awkwardly on cement blocks with broken windows and garbage cans and trash surrounding the place. Looking around, I realized this was a migrant camp. I could hear many voices inside and a dog barking.

Sal turned to me and said, "This is where I live with my family. We live with my aunts, uncles and cousins; fourteen of us. Papa says we are the lucky ones; we have each other."

I smiled in the dark. "He's right, you are lucky."

As he got out of the car, he turned and said, "Thanks for being a giving tree and taking me home, Miss."

At that moment, I felt so fortunate. I was blessed to learn about his family, my migrant students and how they lived.

My amusing stage star was also a hard-working farm worker and lived in a camp. I discovered that Sal contributed to the care and well-being of his family and helped support his brother and sisters. The two nights he was in the play, he could have been working the farms.

My belief in what it really means to be a teacher was transformed in that moment. When I told my mother about the camps, we cleaned out my seven brothers' and sisters' closets. We gathered items of new and used clothing and shoes and I piled everything into the back of my hatchback.

On Friday afternoons, the bell would ring at exactly 3:00 and I would go to my car and lift that hatchback for my "Free Garage Sale." Girls and boys who needed clothes and shoes would politely take what they needed. Other teachers also contributed new and used items.

Sometimes, a student would pull out a sweater and ask, "Miss, can I take this for my mom? She really needs a warm sweater."

Another would say, "Wow, these jeans would fit my dad."

Some would try on the used sneakers to find their size, desperate to find a comfortable pair of shoes. Sal helped organize the shoes and clothing many times. He also helped me start a "blanket drive" when the weather cooled.

One day, the principal called me to his office and I nervously walked down the hall wondering, What have I done?

As I entered the office, I was stunned to see cardboard boxes full of the biggest potatoes and juiciest, red tomatoes I had ever seen! On the boxes, written in black letters were the words, "Thank you, Miss, Thank you." They wanted to give back something to me, but *they* were the true giving trees.

Years have passed, but I will always remember the new shoes we gave Sal and the loving hugs his family gave me, along with glorious vegetables. My heart was forever changed. When Sal revealed the needs in my own community, I believe this was the moment Laces of Love truly began. This experience changed my life forever. I'm convinced that students who receive Laces of Love shoes will take more confident and comfortable strides into their future.

The Happiest Day of My Life

The Laces of Love® website is often full of emails from teachers, school nurses, and shelters requesting shoes for needy children. After making deliveries to several schools early one morning, I was thrilled to get a phone call requesting me to substitute teach for a few days in a third grade classroom. I was excited to meet my class as I entered the school courtyard.

Suddenly I heard a familiar voice. "Hey, Mrs. Nealon! Shoe Lady! I need you over here." The school counselor, Miss Cole, waved me over to a school bench and gave me the adult nod toward the student nearby.

Sitting on the bench was a petite girl with a head full of tiny braids. Next to her was the Laces of Love bag and a pair of new shoes I had delivered to the school. The little girl smiled and looked up at me through her glasses and said, "I hear you are the Laces of Love shoe person."

I laughed. "Yes, that's me, the Shoe Lady!" Reaching down to pull the new shoes from the bag I said, "Let's try your new shoes on and see how they fit!"

I noticed her sore toes popping out through the torn material on the top of her old shoes. Tugging the old shoes off, I was shocked by the threadbare socks that offered no protection. She noticed the tears slipping down my face.

Bright eyes sparkling, she looked at me and said, "Why are you crying? This is the happiest day of my life!"

I put fresh socks and new shoes on her feet and she stood up to admire her appearance.

She touched my shoulder. "These are perfect! My mom will be so glad. This really is the happiest day of my life."

What a gift; I had the privilege of sharing the happiest day of her life.

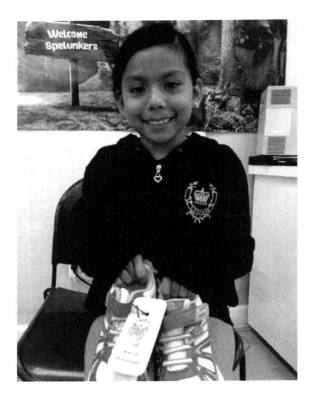

Angela was thrilled with her brand new shoes.
She said they made her feel pretty.

It's not how much we give but how much love we put into giving.
~*St. Teresa of Calcutta*

Prince

His skin was light brown and his arms strong. His smile stretched across his face and his black hair curled around his neck. At six-foot-four, one hundred ninety pounds, they called him Prince of the stadium.

He was an extraordinary football player for fifteen. His natural talent carried him to success as a sophomore on the varsity high school team. He excelled, set records, and continued to impress fans, teammates, and coaches. No one knew that Prince had a secret.

His mother struggled to put food on the table for five children. She recently was laid off from her job and feared losing the apartment. Prince shared his football cleats with his young cousin who played freshman ball.

"We're so lucky," Prince explained to his mom. "The freshman games are on Thursday and I play my varsity games on Friday nights, so we can share the cleats."

Prince didn't care that his foot size was 11 and his cousin's football cleats were size 9½. He didn't care as long as he could play football and run on that field.

Coach would often tell his team, "Prince works hard and gives 100 percent every day. We all need to give that much effort and we can have a winning season."

He was kicked, punched, hit, tackled and clobbered on the practice field and never complained even though he was always running in football cleats that were much too small for his large feet. Prince wore second-hand clothes, but on Friday nights he donned a gold and black jersey—his varsity football uniform—and walked to the field proudly to play for his school.

When the team had away games, the bus would pull into a fast-food restaurant for the players to eat. Many times, Prince would sit quietly on the bus alone. He didn't have money in his pocket, not even loose change.

"I'm too tired," he would say to the others as they quickly rushed off the bus. Sitting alone on the bus, his stomach groaned and grumbled.

When you met Prince, his size would startle you, but his smile was what you remembered. The coach presented Prince with new cleats and a new pair of tennis shoes from Laces of Love®. Prince twirled the Laces of Love tags. "Coach, they're brand new! Can I try them on?" he asked with excitement.

"Sure, they're yours." Coach watched Prince push his foot into the first shoe.

"Coach, they feel great, I'm going to run so fast." Suddenly, Prince stopped and for a moment, just sat in disbelief.

Moments later, my cell phone rang as I was pulling up to the school gate.

The coach's voice was loud and excited. "Hey, Jeanne, where are you? Did you leave the school already?"

Bewildered, I replied, "No, I'm at the gate, what's going on, Coach?"

"Stay right where you are, but turn and look toward the football field."

I glanced over to the high school football field and noticed a huge football player, long legs pumping toward me at full speed. In moments, he vaulted over the gate, with his shiny new football cleats on his feet and another pair of shoes dangling from his neck.

Getting out of my car, I watched Prince continue to steam across the parking lot like a race car. I had no idea what was in store for me. The encounter is one I will never forget.

Prince stopped, winded, took a deep breath and said, "Miss, thank you so much for the shoes and the football cleats." He took the shoes from around his neck and held them close to his chest. "These are awesome; I've never had anything new before." He started to tear up. "Miss, I am going to work so hard. I am going to try my best in school and make good grades." Prince took a deep breath and looked at me gratefully. "I promise, Miss, I will always remember these shoes as the best gift I've ever received."

I cried all the way home.

The wrestling team at Lely High School (Collier County) receiving their wrestling shoes.

Crowded Quarters

When I was invited to ride with the migrant resource teachers on the home visits, I was a bit hesitant and had many questions. I had been to migrant camps in the past and, since 1981, had many migrant students in my classroom.

The resource teacher explained, "You will see the devastation up close and it becomes very personal. Many times we see the home in distress and filth. Can you handle it?"

"Yes, I want to meet the people who need help," I answered from the back of the school van. It was the early days of Laces of Love®. The charity had already given to many schools in this particular area of our county.

Pulling up into the trailer park, I couldn't believe my eyes. Chipped paint, falling pieces of metal, broken screen doors hanging from the last hinge, tall weeds, steps made haphazardly of old pallets to the entrances of the broken-down trailers, and trash.

The van circled the dirty road around the corner to our first stop. As we pulled in close to the trailer, the driver had to squeeze into a parking space between a broken-down old truck, garbage stacked inside plastic discarded bins, and old furniture. Outside the trailer sat two potted plants with beautiful pink flowers and four old metal lawn chairs seated in a circle.

The resource teacher explained. "They work at landscape businesses and are given flowers many times at work." I followed the two teachers to the side of the trailer.

As one teacher knocked on the door, I glanced around again noticing broken plastic toys scattered about and a tiny, plastic child's swimming pool turned upside down in the dirt.

"*Hola!*" A tiny dark-skinned woman opened the door, smiled, and invited us into her home.

We sat around a long metal table with a tiny jar of small flowers in the middle. The table was chipped on the surface and it wobbled when anyone leaned on it. The woman and the resource teachers discussed many things in Spanish. I know very little of the language but could pick up the gist of the conversation.

How are you doing? How is your husband's job? Are your children happy in school? Do you have any questions concerning your children's teachers?

The teachers asked many questions concerning the well-being of the children. One of their primary objectives for home visits is to find out what is going on in the home and what help is needed.

As I listened to their voices, I was taken aback by the conditions; the old tiny, beat-up trailer with paint chipping off the inside walls, paneling boards missing everywhere, electric light bulbs with small chains dangling from loose wires above. The kitchen sink was fitted with a large piece of wood, pipes exposed with plumbing wrapped around the side of the kitchen. Clean pots were stacked on a tiny wood shelf and a little dishrag hung on a knob above the sink. There was no refrigerator or any appliance for that matter. It was hard not to cry.

"Do you have any questions for Maria?" the resource teacher asked.

I was startled by her tap on my arm. "Yes, yes. How many children do you have? What do you need? Do you live in this home alone? Where does your husband work? How can I help?"

As I waited for the resource teacher to translate to her, I noticed the mama's brown eyes were kind as she listened and looked back and forth at me and the other teachers.

Her answers stunned me. She said she had four children and her husband to take care of, but they live with four other people. She pointed to the two doors on the other side of the kitchen table and explained they rented the trailer with four other men. Two of the men sleep in one room and the other two men share the second room. She and her husband and four children share one bathroom with these four men. She said two of the men are her husband's cousins, but the other two men work with her neighbor and they needed a place to live. They pay $950 a month for this trailer with ten people living in this small place.

Speaking to me in English the teacher said, "It goes on all the time; ten to twelve people live in horrible conditions trying to survive paycheck to paycheck, farm to farm. However, they are happy to be able to work and happy their children can attend school."

Mother, husband, and four children sleep in the same cramped space; all their belongings piled high in one corner, worn sleeping bags lying across one bed while another make-shift bed stood in the corner.

The mother smiled. "I'm happy to be here where my children can go to school. It is a good life. We can work and we have a place to stay. We can forget the life we left behind."

I admired her desire and appreciation for the chance to work and help her children have a better life. She asked for simple things for her children; shoes and clothing. Sitting there at the table, I knew I could help her and I wanted to help. Extremely poor people that desire nothing but goodness for their children and a good life is something to be admired. Her home was not a broken-down trailer, her home was the love that lives in her heart for her family.

Tamika's Noisy Shoes

Tamika was a highly social fifth-grader who walked confidently through the halls of her elementary school. She had a unique sense of style and choice of outfits. Her grandmother's old beaded sweater tied around her shoulders, discarded old shoe laces wrapped around her hair in braids, and two different colored stockings made up her special look.

One day, Tamika appeared in the school office wearing an unusual pair of shoes. As she walked over to the front desk, her high heels clicked and tapped on the school floor. *Clunk, tap. Click, tap. Thunk, tap.* Everyone stopped to watch Tamika wobble around on very high-heeled shoes.

"Tamika, those high heels are not suitable for school," the school secretary scolded.

"They're the only shoes I have to wear," Tamika explained. "My tennis shoes are too small and they hurt my feet. My mom's friend gave me these shoes to wear." She continued to plead in a delicate voice, "I know they're different, but I have no other shoes."

The secretary looked at the high heels and shook her head. "I'm going to give you a warning, but get some different shoes as soon as possible. High heels aren't allowed in school."

Tamika clacked her way out of the school office and down the hall. She tucked the yellow warning note into her book-bag and tried to walk, but had only gone a few steps when she tripped and fell. A teacher hurried over to help her up and glanced down at the high heels.

The teacher pulled a yellow tablet from his pocket along with a red pen and wrote up a warning citation for dress code. He tore the yellow sheet from the pad and handed it to her. "You can't wear those shoes to school!"

Struggling to stand up, Tamika said, "I don't have any other..." But he was already walking away.

She tucked the second warning slip into her book-bag and tried again to walk. *Tap, clunk.* Her toes were pinched and her feet were throbbing. She stopped and looked down at her shoes in frustration.

Slipping behind a hallway door, Tamika tried to hide for a moment. The bell rang and children rushed to their classrooms. She tried to run, but her left heel caught in the metal threshold and broke right off. Now, she was wearing only one high heel and a broken shoe. Tamika was limping when the last teacher found her. She collapsed and started to cry.

"I have nothing else to wear on my feet but these old cracked high heels." Her legs stretched out on the floor as the teacher pulled the shoes off. Her frail toes were able to stretch and wiggle. Relief came across Tamika's face. "Those shoes were killing me!"

The teacher reassured her gently, "Trust me, we'll find you a new pair of shoes that will fit perfectly."

Moments later, Tamika was fitted with a brand new pair of Laces of Love® shoes, and her gratitude was overflowing. "Thank you so much! They fit and they're beautiful. My feet don't hurt now."

Then, Tamika paused and a strange sorrow crossed her face. "Can I wear the shoes home or do they stay at school?"

"Honey, those are your very own shoes to keep forever."

Tamika gave the teacher a big hug. "I can't believe they are truly my shoes to keep!"

For a very long time, the teacher kept the broken pair of high heels in her classroom closet to remind her of Tamika and the brand new Laces of Love shoes that fit perfectly.

New shoes inspire students like Cleo to work harder in school as well as to play sports.

My Brand New Feet

Emmanuel was a very happy child and was always eager to please his first grade teacher. He volunteered to collect papers, pass out books, or sharpen pencils. Whatever his teacher needed, he was right there, waving his hand eagerly and ready to help.

One morning she noticed that Emmanuel limped through the door.

"Hey, my friend, what's wrong?" she asked. "Why are you limping?"

As he struggled to walk toward his teacher, he looked up at her with a sorrowful expression. "My feet hurt."

She took him into her office, knelt down beside him and tried to take off his old shoes. They were so tight that she had to unlace them completely to get them off.

Inside, his sweaty, tattered socks shed pieces of sand and dirt to the floor when she pulled them off. Emmanuel winced as the socks revealed badly swollen feet.

"I think they're too tight for me." He wiggled his bare toes in relief. "My mom is going to get a new job soon and buy me new shoes," he explained.

Emmanuel's family had been living in a shelter for the past several months and he had been wearing the same pair of old shoes for a very long time.

His teacher went to her closet for a minute. Emmanuel's eyes grew bright with excitement when he saw what she pulled out. In her hands was a pair of Laces of Love® shoes with a new pair of socks tucked inside them. She gently placed them onto Emmanuel's swollen feet. He sat quietly while she slid the new shoes on.

Suddenly, Emmanuel jumped up, bouncing around the room. "Look, everyone," he shouted, "I have brand new feet!"

His teacher asked the office to check on his older sister and her shoe needs, and she was excited to replace her worn-out shoes with a new pair, too. When he saw his sister's shoes, Emmanuel shouted, "Look, you have brand new feet, too!"

Skipping

I arrived early on a record-cold January morning and noticed Alicia shivering on a cement block near the school parking lot. She wore a short-sleeved t-shirt, torn jeans, but no jacket. Beside her was a well-worn backpack with a broken strap.

"Hey, what's wrong? Why are you sitting outside in this freezing weather?"

Although she was reluctant to answer, she finally said, "I lost my shoe, I can't find it anywhere. How can I go to school with only one shoe?" Tears slid down her face in embarrassment. "I can't find my other blue tennis shoe."

I looked down at Alicia's old tattered blue shoe on one foot and a worn, thread-bare sock on the other. Her wild, curly hair contradicted the despair in her brown eyes. I reflected on the courage it must have taken her to hobble all the way to school with one foot bare on that chilly morning.

"Alicia, come with me." She put her small hand in mine and walked awkwardly, tip-toeing and hopping to keep her shoeless toes on the cold cement as little as possible while her other foot did the walking work.

She continued to weep as we neared the school office. "Am I in trouble?"

I shook my head and pointed at the row of brand-new Laces of Love® shoes in the closet. Alicia looked at them in wonder then back at me. She started to smile and finally let go of my hand.

I found a brightly-colored pair that perfectly fit Alicia's small feet along with new socks. She wiped away her tears and beamed as she turned this way and that to look at her new shoes.

"Thank you, Miss! Thank you!" I watched her skipping with a joyful heart all the way down the hall. After experiencing this little miracle on that cold January day, I felt like skipping, too!

A Laces of Love shoe drive with Ashlie and Kyle Chapman, and Laces Co-founder, Jeanne Nealon.

Run Away Soles

As a guidance counselor, I've seen an increase in previously solid, middle-class families who are losing their jobs, their cars and their homes. Laces of Love® is helping students who never thought they would require assistance. We are so grateful for your support for our needy kids. Here's just one example:

Senior cross-country runner, Mike, wore an old pair of shoes he said he found at work one day; beat-up, torn, with the soles unhinged from the tops.

Mike tried to explain his running shoes. "They're Adrenalines, Coach, my favorite kind of trainers."

All Coach could hear was a flapping noise whenever Mike took a step and he knew Mike needed help. This kid gives his all, he thought. He attends school full-time, works part-time in a restaurant to cover food, clothing, car, and school expenses for himself and his younger sister. He'd never let you know that he went without breakfast and lunch to have enough money to pay for his sister's school clothes, or fix the alternator on his beat up old car, which he needed to get back and forth to work.

One afternoon before practice, Coach called Mike into the athletic office to give him new training shoes for cross-country. Tears welled up in the runner's eyes as he opened the box and saw the Laces of Love tag. Not only was he excited to get a new pair of running shoes, he was stunned to receive new sneakers for both himself and his sister for school.

You enabled us to help an ambitious young man have a great season. Every day since Mike received his new shoes, he waits until after all the other kids leave to say, thank you. He thanks the Laces of Love group that cared enough to provide the shoes he'd never ask for, but desperately needed.

Thank you so much,

High School Guidance Counselor and Cross-Country Coach

It's Your Lucky Day

It was a cloudy day when ten-year-old Renaldo headed off to school. He thought he could beat the storm, if his bulky shoes cooperated. The Youth Relations Officer had taped them together for him yesterday and, hopefully, they would not fall apart on his walk to school. Renaldo's mom could not afford to buy him new shoes, so she made him wear his father's old work shoes, the only thing he left behind when he abandoned them months ago.

His father's shoes were size 10 and Renaldo wore a 5. He would often complain to his mom. "These shoes are too big, too long, too wide and too loose. Please, I need new shoes."

Embarrassed, Renaldo would often hide his clunky, big shoes under his school desk. Kids would laugh and say, "Renaldo, where did you get those clown shoes? You can use them as canoes."

He often hid in a corner at school as his feelings of despair intensified.

On this day, the sky darkened and Renaldo felt the first heavy drops of rain fall on his shoulders. He tried to dash for the school entrance, but the over-sized shoes caused him to stumble down the sidewalk. A strong gust of wind pushed him along as he pulled his dripping jacket tight.

"You're almost there, you're almost there," he told himself. He continued down toward the side entrance, pulling his jacket up over his head against the rain.

A harsh voice came from the doorway. "Stop! Where do you think you are going? Students enter from the back."

He could barely see in the rain, but the stern voice was enough to move him on his way. He rushed down the sidewalk to take cover under the bus awning.

Another voice shouted. "You can't stay here! This is for bus riders only. Move out of the way!" This angry voice was wearing a hooded raincoat and held a fancy umbrella. Renaldo wanted to be a fish in the gurgling gutter and swim away.

A squishy sucking sound accompanied him as his drenched socks clung to his cold feet inside his shoes. Renaldo huddled alone under the bike rack sign, waiting for the bell to ring. His pants and feet were soaked, his heart burdened, and he shivered uncontrollably.

Looking down at him with disapproval another voice ordered, "What are you doing here? Get out of the bike rack." The arm pointed him in another direction and he was left standing in the rain again. Renaldo wandered off to the side schoolyard. Everything was going wrong this morning. He shriveled up into a corner of the playground under a tree, feeling helpless and alone.

Suddenly he heard a trusted voice. "Renaldo, my man!"

It was the Youth Relations Officer, Deputy Amos, holding a huge orange umbrella and wearing a big grin.

"Come on, buddy! Get under here with me." Deputy Amos grabbed Renaldo and sheltered him under the umbrella as they walked quickly down the sidewalk leading to the office.

"What were you doing out there by yourself?" Deputy Amos shook off the umbrella as they entered the school.

"W-waiting for the first b-bell to ring," Renaldo stammered, peeling off his wet jacket as he slogged slowly down the hall with Deputy Amos.

Just then, a loud bell rang. Simultaneously, Deputy Amos and Renaldo laughed and said, "There's the first bell!"

Deputy Amos tried to dry off Renaldo's hair with a towel he found in the clinic and said, "I called this special group about getting you a new pair of shoes."

Renaldo, shivering with cold, started to cry. "These are the only s-shoes I h-have to wear, b-but they're too b-b-big for my feet."

The deputy put a reassuring hand on his shoulder. "I promise you that today you will be wearing new shoes!"

Just then, the school office door blew open with the wind and rain in torrents.

"Renaldo, this is your lucky day!"

Renaldo raised his eyebrows in question.

Deputy Amos smiled and pointed to the door. "Look, the Shoe Lady has just arrived with your brand new shoes!"

Renaldo jumped up to look at his new shoes and then shouted, "Wow, it is my lucky day after all!"

Impossible situations can become possible miracles.

~*Robert H. Schuller*

Dear Laces of Love,

Our elementary school has a very high percentage of Guatemalan families. Many mothers will walk to school daily with their very young children. The mothers wear long formal skirts and mismatched tops, with old high heels on their feet. Some will walk miles to the Salvation Army for lunch to get food for their children.

Last month, one little girl had nothing to wear on her feet but an old pair of high heels. These shoes made it impossible for this little girl to walk down the school hallway. We were able to bring her quietly into our school clinic and fit her with her first pair of new sneakers. She spoke very little English, but after looking down at her pink shoelaces, she just jumped into my arms and gave me a hug! Thank you laces of love.

School Nurse

The Morning Walkers

Mrs. Bloom greeted me in the school office when I arrived that Monday morning. "Jeanne, you'll be featured on our morning news and the kids can't wait! Our parent volunteers will hear you speak at the breakfast in a little while."

This was one of many elementary schools in great need. Seventy-five percent of the students are on free or reduced lunch and are identified as economically disadvantaged. Laces of Love® had distributed shoes to many children at this school and they invited me to receive a small award from their students.

"First, please come with me." Mrs. Bloom was dressed in a cute modern spring dress with a purple scarf around her shoulders. Following her down the hall, I noticed the bright sneakers on her feet. She zipped out the side door toward the blacktop full of students. "Hurry, we have exactly 20 minutes before the morning news begins and the kids do their morning walk on the far field." Her voice was excited as she moved quickly to the field and I followed.

"Hi, Mrs. Bloom!" a student shouted from a distance.

"Mrs. Bloom, are we walking the field today?" a young boy with striped shorts joined us by her side.

"Mrs. Bloom, where is our guest? We've been waiting for the lady with shoes." A slender girl with glasses ran alongside Mrs. Bloom.

After arriving at the far field, I was greeted by many students all wearing familiar sneakers; shoes that traveled from donors to my garage to their school, and were now worn happily by so many students.

Mrs. Bloom directed me toward the exercise trail and we started our walk. I had no idea this would be the *best* walk of my life. We started slow and Mrs. Bloom began telling me how much Laces of Love has changed lives at their school. I was trying to keep up with her pace, and suddenly a student arrived right next to me.

We continued to walk, escorted by this young man with dimples.

"Hi!" he said. "Mrs. Bloom told me that you gave me my shoes. I just wanted to say thanks." He wiggled his feet into the ground a bit and then smiled.

Just as I was about to introduce myself, two brothers raced up and jumped in the air in front of us.

"Hey, we love our shoes. Thank you for having Laces of Love donate to our school. Mom and Dad were so happy when we got our shoes at school."

Next a small young man around eight years old and carrying a large book bag approached us. "I like my shoes," he said. "Mrs. Bloom said you are the lady with the shoes. Thanks a lot for my new shoes, they're comfortable."

Another young girl ran up along side me as I continued to walk the trail.

"Miss! Miss! Can I just tell you how much it means to me getting my new shoes? I was wearing my sister's shoes from last year. They didn't fit my feet and I had to curl my toes in as I squeezed into my shoes each day. Then, Mrs. Bloom called me into her office and gave me this new pair of blue shoes!"

She reached up and gave me the biggest hug. Her shoes were beautiful and her smile radiated appreciation. She continued to walk next to me as many other children greeted me and thanked me for their shoes. Surprised and stunned to meet so many children with Laces of Love shoes on their feet, I was moved to tears. The children surrounded me as I walked the path ever so slowly now.

Many of the children were chanting and singing, "We love our shoes. We love our shoes."

The excitement continued with each step of the trail. The love and enthusiasm was growing in their faces. They started to line up around the trail as a celebration. Many children with new shoes were clapping, singing, and cheering along the path.

A girl with frizzy black hair tied in a pink ribbon raced towards me. "I was in a real jam, Miss," she said. "I didn't know what I was going to do the day my boots broke. The zipper on my boots came completely apart and my boots were torn on both sides. I cried in the school bathroom until Mrs. Bloom gave me a new pair of shoes to wear. Laces of Love saved my life. My mom said that we couldn't afford new shoes the day my boot zipper came apart. You saved my life!" Her smile beamed and she ran as fast as she could halfway around the trail in her new shoes.

Mrs. Bloom explained about these morning walkers to me. "These are children who come to school exceptionally early because their parents catch public transportation to go to work. We designated this early drop off time as an exercise program and they are referred to as the Morning Walkers. Take a look around this trail, because Laces of Love has helped all of them."

The Morning Walkers shared hugs, handshakes, and love all along the trail with me that day. This was a spiritual experience for me as my heart pounded with each step and each "thank you" from the students. The morning walkers fueled my energy to keep going, to continue the mission to give and give to children in need.

This trail was a celebration of love and joy and confirmation that Laces of Love is on the right path.

The Dance

After delivering several bags of shoes to the elementary school, the office manager stopped me in the hall. Her eyes gleamed with excitement. "Come over to the window and I'll show you a student who received new shoes yesterday."

She gestured at the fenced playground where the children were starting to line up for the morning bell. Pointing out a curly-headed boy in a green jacket, she turned to me and touched my arm. "He's so happy, he hasn't stopped dancing! Besides providing shoes, Laces of Love is also giving a smile to these children. That little guy hid his feet under the desk because his shoes smelled. When he told his teacher that his feet hurt, she took off his shoes and his feet were raw with sores."

As I walked out to the parking lot, I watched the boy in the green jacket looking down at his new shoes. He hopped, jumped, and danced with joy. All around him children ran and played, but he twirled, swayed and danced on the grassy surface. I thought I had seen everything that new shoes can bring a child, but this was a new moment of magic. You can tell a child is truly happy when he is dancing.

Do You Have Glue?

Study hall after school enables kids to get their homework done or get assistance if they have questions or need materials for projects.

One student was in the study hall for tutoring and said, "Miss, I need some really strong glue."

Assuming he was working on a science project, Miss Rachel told him, "I don't have any super glue, but I have a bottle of regular glue."

He asked, "Do you think that kind will hold leather?"

"Leather?" she asked with a puzzled look.

Scooting away from the table, the young man pointed to his shoes. "The glue's for my shoes. I've tried rubber glue before and it only works for a little while."

Miss Rachel looked down at the pair of cracked, brown, faux leather shoes that had completely fallen apart. She gestured for the young man to follow her to the school nurse's office. She pulled a few pairs of sneakers from the shelf, looked into his shoes for a size and saw it was worn away long ago. "What size do you wear?"

"I'm not sure, I've haven't had a new pair of shoes in a long time, maybe a 5?"

After trying on several pairs of shoes, the young man fit into a men's size 8. He walked proudly around the office testing the feel of his new shoes then gave Miss Rachel a big hug and left with a radiant smile.

As she was about to leave, she saw the boy's teacher standing thoughtfully looking at the floor. The young man's old, cracked shoes sat on the floor near the wall, thankfully, retired and replaced with a brand new pair of sneakers from Laces of Love.

Tyson's Shoe Tags

"Good morning, Mrs. Jenson, nice dress."

"Hey, love the bowtie, Mr. Marks!"

Tyson was a cheerful and busy second grader, nearly eight years old. He complimented his teachers often when he passed them in the halls. His adorable nature carried him along; so did his bulky, big leather shoes.

When it came time for physical education class, Tyson was falling over his feet to get to Coach Parker's class.

"Are we going outside today, Coach? Are we playing kick ball?" He jumped up and down as he continued his daily questions to Coach Parker. "Can I carry the balls, Coach? Do you need any help?" The boy's enthusiasm could fill basketball arenas.

"Hey, Coach, can I carry your clipboard? Can I wear your whistle? Please, give me something to carry, Coach," Tyson pleaded as the other second graders filed into a single line.

His clumsy shoes made him appear awkward at times, but he was a hardy competitor in class despite shoes literally falling off his feet. The other students would make fun of his shoes, but Tyson paid no attention. No matter how difficult his life at home seemed, Tyson carried joy in his back pocket.

Each day, he would stand directly behind Coach Parker and wait eagerly for her to unlock the doors to the equipment room. Wearing a broad smile and hopping from one shoe to the other, he would gaze into the large room with excitement. "Wow, Coach! You have all the stuff anyone could ever dream of—kick balls, hockey sticks, soccer balls, volleyball nets, field bases..."

Just as he would assist his other teachers, Tyson would cheerfully carry the equipment for Coach.

One day, Coach Parker watched Tyson slogging down the hall, slower than usual in his bulky shoes. When Tyson came to class that afternoon, he was surprised to see cool, black running shoes in his Coach's hands.

"Coach, what are those?" he asked.

"Your new shoes, Ty!"

With his mouth wide open, Tyson looked up at Coach Parker in disbelief. "These shoes are for *me*? Can I wear them now?"

Connected to the shoes was a familiar Laces of Love® shoe tag. As he strutted out of the gym that day carrying his old shoes in a bag, Coach Parker watched Tyson twirl the shoe tag on its string.

When she saw Tyson the next day though, he was wearing his old leather shoes again and clutching the Laces of Love bag in his arms. "Ty, why aren't you wearing your new shoes?"

He couldn't hold back the tears. Through hiccups and sobs he said, "My mama...said we...don't...have any extra money...for new shoes and made me...bring them back."

Coach Parker explained that the shoes were a gift from Laces of Love that he could keep.

Hope in his big brown eyes, he asked, "I can keep them? Forever?"

Coach said, "Yes. Those are your new shoes—forever!"

Standing in disbelief, Tyson took the new shoes out of the brown bag and asked again, "Coach, I can keep them? Are they for free?"

"Yes. Those are your new shoes," she replied.

The very next day, Tyson came leaping into the gymnasium and gave Coach a big hug. Around his neck on a piece of yarn was the Laces of Love shoe tag.

Tyson proudly wore his new black tennis shoes and showed the tag to Coach. "Look, Coach Parker, look what my mama wrote on this shoe tag."

Turning the pink Laces of Love shoe tag over, there in big words, Tyson's mom wrote: "We Love Laces of Love! Thank you!" Signed "Tyson's Grateful Mama!"

High Tops for Tender Foot

The phone call was one of many that day. "This is Miss Gina from the elementary school. We need a size 2 for a very young girl and we need them in high tops, please."

I wrote down the message and wondered, Why high tops? High tops are basketball shoes that are large on the sides of your foot and cost more. We purchase high tops for high school basketball players in need, but why does a little girl need high top basketball shoes? They are hard to find and can be very expensive.

I decided to contact Miss Gina and ask her a few questions about this unusual request. "The request for size 2 high tops is for Cynthia, a little girl in the special needs program. She has a syndrome called *Cri Du Chat* and struggles to walk so she scoots across the floor. She wears out the sides of her shoes very quickly from scooting. She has braces and the high tops could provide her the support she needs as we slide the braces into the sides of her shoes."

I held the phone out and gasped. I had questioned why she needed this special request and now I wanted to give her several new pairs of high tops in every rainbow color!

The teacher further explained how this student tries to walk and needs the high-top shoes to support her weak legs. "She wobbles from side to side and each step requires tremendous strength and courage. She scoots across the classroom floor and gains strength. Then she tries to pull herself up to standing position and attempts to move a few brief steps forward. She moves along by gripping my hand, but her days are not predictable; she faces obstacles and is easily frustrated."

I ran to the store and found a beautiful pair of pink size 2 high-top basketball shoes for Cynthia. When her new shoes arrived at school, she became very excited according to the teacher.

"When we pulled the shoes from the box, Cynthia's face showed her joy. She bounced her legs up and down and made little noises of celebration!"

Her teachers felt confident that the new pink shoes were a fantastic stimulation for Cynthia. She often looks down at her shoes and twirls the pink shoestrings. Each step Cynthia takes is a moment of courage. When she scoots across the carpet, her bright eyes communicate happiness and light up the entire classroom. The other children know Cynthia is scooting towards them and they cheer her on until she reaches her destination across the room.

"Although she doesn't make a lot of noise, her courage and cheerful enthusiasm spreads love to everyone she sees. Cynthia loves her new pink high top shoes. She's our 'tender foot'."

Do not wait for leaders; do it alone, person to person.
~*St. Teresa of Calcutta*

Right on Target

"Wow, now that's a ton of shoes!" The jolly sales clerk grinned and chuckled as he started to unload the carts. He delighted in helping me with the shoes and made funny conversation.

"So, you must have a lot of kids!" he said with a smile and chuckled to himself.

The cashier looked at him. "Andy, you know this is for a charitable foundation!" The older woman smiled at me and continued to ring up the shoes on her register while snapping her chewing gum. "I've checked out your shoe charity many times at this register."

For every two pairs of shoes that I pulled from the cart, Andy quickly grabbed five or six pairs and tossed them onto the moving conveyor belt for check out. His light-hearted personality and jokes make me grin.

"We're just whizzing through this purchase! We should be done with this shoe transaction by lunchtime—tomorrow!" He laughed infectiously.

He separated the colors and sizes and put similar shoes together and helped to organize them into the bags. Then, Andy asked me a question. "So where do these new shoes go exactly?"

"We deliver to all the schools and to shelters as well."

"Do you deliver to high schools, too?" Andy asked.

"Yes, we deliver a lot of shoes to the high schools and also we deliver athletic shoes for sports."

Andy was so polite and kind-hearted; I was drawn to his fun personality.

"I'd like to help you get the shoes loaded into your car."

After paying the bill, I pushed one cart and Andy followed me with two more. Pushing the carts steadily toward my car, I noticed Andy get a little quiet for a moment. I looked back to see if he was still following.

"Oh my gosh! I just realized something. This is Laces of Love, right?" he asked as he looked at the poster in the back of my trunk.

"Yes," I answered as we unloaded the carts and stuffed the bags of shoes into my car.

Andy stopped and just looked at me. "I owe you the biggest thank you. You guys gave me shoes when I really needed them in high school. I wear a size thirteen and you helped me out."

I looked up at this wonderful Target® sales clerk and he gave me the biggest hug. He reached down into his pocket and pulled out a ten-dollar bill and handed it to me.

"I know this isn't much, but please use it toward a pair of shoes for a kid in school."

Driving away from the Target® parking lot, I felt an Andy quip coming on. *He'd say that I was right on Target!*

> "The most beautiful things in the world cannot be seen or touched, they are felt with the heart."
>
> ~*Antoine de Saint-Exupéry,*
> from *The Little Prince*

We Have the Same Name?

There was a knock on the classroom door and the students looked up from their tests. The guidance counselor smiled and beckoned me to come to the back of the room.

"The students are taking a quiz and I'm the sub today," I whispered.

She smiled. "I know, but I want you to do something for me. I'll watch your class while you give out the shoes you delivered yesterday to our school."

I looked out into the hallway and sitting on the floor was our Laces of Love® brown paper bag containing three pairs of new shoes. Then I heard some giggling near the door. Standing in a neat row were three little boys wearing smiles.

The counselor pushed me gently into the hall and closed the door.

Being the co-founder, president, and speaker for Laces of Love, I rarely give the new shoes directly to the children. Now, because of the kindness of this counselor, I was given this special opportunity.

The three boys looked at me with their big brown eyes and continued to smile. I reached into the bag and pulled out one of the pairs of shoes I had brought to the school the day before.

"Size 5." I smiled as I read the size out loud. "Who wears a size 5?"

"I could try them on," said the tallest boy who was in third grade. He sat on the floor with me and struggled with the dirty old pair—a size 3.

I put his new size 5 shoes on his feet and they fit perfectly.

"Wow!" he shouted. "These feel really good on my feet." He stood up and raced around in circles in the hallway.

"What's your name?" I asked the tall young boy.

"I'm Ricardo," he said joyfully. "Ricardo, the boy with new shoes now!"

The next young man already had his shoes off and was waiting patiently. I pulled a red and white pair from the bag and said, "Size 2, hmmm, they look just your size." I smiled and helped him put the new shoes on his feet.

His eyes were wide as I laced the tennis shoes. He stood up and started to dance around a bit and then leaped down the hall.

He giggled. "Look, Ricardo! Look at me! I can jump really high in these new shoes!"

"What's your name?" I asked.

"My name is Arturo. My mom is going to be so happy I have new shoes." He stood and cocked his head from side to side to admire his new shoes.

"Okay, we have one more pair of shoes left in the bag." I slowly reached in and pulled size 12½ shoes from the Laces of Love bag.

Ricardo and Arturo stood very still and watched me put the new shoes on the smallest boy in the hallway. The boy stood and shifted back and forth on his feet.

"Do they fit?" asked Ricardo.

The child just beamed.

As I looked up at him, I asked, "What's your name?"

The little boy just grinned at me with wonder and joy on his face.

I asked him again, "And, what is your name?"

His long eyelashes dusted the tops of his cheeks with each blink, but he didn't answer.

Ricardo and Arturo reached down to me and put their arms on my shoulders and said, "Miss, his name is the same as your name."

Confused, I smiled and asked, "Really?"

"Yes, he has your name. His name is Angel."

Goody Two Shoes

My niece participates in a wonderful program called Special Olympics. She's often told me about her sporting events and weekly practices and I was always invited to attend. This particular spring, my schedule and workload lightened and I was able to go to several of her basketball practices. She played with the high school and upper level leagues. Walking into the gym that very first time, I was surprised at the enthusiastic reception I received.

One boisterous and fun-loving young man named Phillip greeted me. "Hey, you're the Shoe Lady!" His voice was loud and his face was bright and cheery.

I realized my niece had told the world about her aunt and Laces of Love®. She introduced me to everyone: her teammates, her coaches, her life skills mentor, and many other volunteers at that practice session. She loved her practices and I enjoyed watching her run up and down the court. With three brothers, she was more than capable of stealing the ball and shooting baskets!

Several parents confided in me and I learned of a great need. Many of the players were wearing second-hand shoes and some kids were in the Foster Care System. Over the years, Laces of Love has helped many special needs children by fitting them in proper shoes for their sizes and individual foot issues. Some of the parents told me that Laces of Love had helped their children receive shoes at their schools. I noticed my new friend,

Phillip, struggled to run up and down the court in his shoes. He was not able to keep his balance and often stumbled over his own feet.

One parent said, "Oh Jeanne, the support of a high top sneaker basketball shoe would be great for our kids!"

Some of the parents that could afford to purchase basketball shoes for their special needs children made donations to Laces of Love and handed me checks and money that day to help the other kids on the team. Their generosity was overwhelming.

As I measured their feet at the next practice, my niece hovered over my shoulder and told me individual stories about each of her special friends. Then Phillip was next in line.

"Phillip is a great basketball player and one of my best friends!" My niece giggled as she talked about him.

Other kids spoke up:

"My dad says Phillip is good but does not share the ball!"

"He makes all the baskets for our team, but he does not like to pass us the ball."

With his big voice Philip said, "Hey, Shoe Lady. I am a shooter. I shoot the baskets. I get the basketball and I shoot the baskets!"

I measured Phillip's feet that day and realized he was wearing a pair of shoes with a VELCRO® strap.

"Hey, Shoe Lady," he said. "I only wear VELCRO. I only wear VELCRO shoes."

I smiled and jotted his foot size down on my notepad. It will be difficult to find a large men's size basketball shoe with VELCRO fasteners, I thought.

Tapping me on my shoulder, Phillip insisted, "Shoe Lady, I only wear VELCRO!" He was asking me for a confirmation that he was going to receive a new pair of shoes with VELCRO® fasteners.

Looking at his friendly face, I said, "How about if I get you a pair of school shoes that have VELCRO and another pair for basketball? You need the support of a basketball shoe and your feet will feel secure and strong while you run up and down the court."

Pouting, Phillip turned to me and insisted, "I only wear VELCRO!"

In a hushed voice I continued, "Phillip, if you can keep a secret I'll get you two pairs of shoes."

"A secret?" Phillip shouted and his voice rang through the gym. We burst out laughing together.

The next moment, Phillip leaned close to me and cupped my ear, with his hands, and then he tried to whisper, "If you give me two pairs of shoes and one pair has VELCRO, I won't tell anyone!"

* * *

The Special Olympics Coach was thrilled the day we arrived with the new shoes for the players. I was proud to thank the parents who supported our Laces of Love purchases. Lacing up Phillip's basketball shoes, I sensed he was disappointed.

Looking at me with a serious face he asked, "Where are my VELCRO shoes?"

Reaching behind my chair, I pulled out the Laces of Love bag to show him the other hidden pair of new shoes —with the VELCRO® fasteners he requested.

Looking into the bag, his eyes grew wide and a big smile flashed across his face. "VELCRO shoes!" He immediately caught himself and reminded me, "I know,

Shoe Lady, I won't tell anyone you gave me two pairs of shoes. Goody, Goody, two shoes for Phillip!"

My niece waved to me as she entered the court in her red and white uniform. The players were all dressed in their new shoes and they continued to gaze at each other's feet as they were introduced. Sitting in the wooden bleachers with my sister, we waited eagerly for the game to start.

As were all the other games that season, this one was also full of fun and laughter. The players worked hard, and the fans cheered and encouraged both teams as they competed on the basketball court. I was surprised as Phillip made several steals and successful shots at the basket. He loved shooting and loved his team—and he was even learning how to share the ball.

During the game, he noticed me sitting in the stands and shouted, "Hey, Shoe Lady!"

He loved calling me that. He played his game, but at one point he was traveling down the court, his eyes focused on the basket, and suddenly stopped at half court, right in front of me. Tucking the basketball under his arm, he looked up at me and shouted, "Don't worry Shoe Lady, I can keep a secret and won't tell anybody you gave me two pairs of shoes!"

The crowd burst into laughter and Phillip continued down the court to score again. All I could think of was, *Goody, goody, two shoes!*

The miracle is this—the more we share, the more we have.
~Leonard Nimoy

Walk in Her Shoes

Rushing into the department store, I quickly pulled two carts apart and rolled them down the crowded aisle, jetting toward the shoe department. Nothing special that day, just ordinary shoe shopping for Laces of Love® to fill shoe requests as they came into our website. I had several little sizes, but needed the larger size shoes for the middle school and high school students in need. Passing other customers, I drove the shopping carts with purpose.

I caught a glimpse of a thin woman wearing a soft pink head scarf in the corner of the shoe department who was looking my way, but I was on a mission and had a lot to get done. I continued down the aisle, arrived at the section full of women's sizes, and quickly scanned the shelves.

I opened shoe boxes, checking the sizes and making sure there was both a left and a right shoe. This selection is great, I thought, and the 30 percent off sign makes my day. I gazed down the aisle and again saw the woman in the pink scarf. I continued to check sizes and toss the shoes into my carts. After clearing the shelves in this section, I moved on to find more shoes. Beginning the process all over again in the next aisle, I squatted down by the bottom shelf. I'd done this hundreds of times; open boxes, check sizes, and toss them into the cart.

The woman in the pink scarf was now standing in the next aisle watching curiously, but she said nothing.

Concentrating on my task and looking for sizes we needed, my goal was searching for bargains. I took out my list then checked what I'd already placed in the cart. Both carts were filling up, but I had another aisle of shoes to check and was running out of time.

Leaving the carts, I jumped up and ran over to the next aisle. Wow, so many good shoes and great prices today! I thought. As I grabbed boxes from the shelves, the same woman moved to stand near me. Ever so softly, she asked, "Can I help you find some sizes?"

I laughed and pointed to the carts. "Yes, I need a lot of sizes today!"

She took a box off the shelf, removed the shoes, checked the sizes, and handed the shoes to me. She was fragile and beautiful and I saw kindness in her eyes. She looked at the empty boxes left on the shelves and asked, "Can I help stack those discarded boxes for you?"

"Sure, that would be great," I said. She had been watching my routine.

She carefully placed her purse in the shopping cart and began to stack the empty boxes. Quietly, she invited me into her life.

"I know you," she said. "I know exactly who you are and what you do." She hesitated then continued, "I'm a mother of three. I'm divorced and last year, well, I got really sick. Cancer. My kids were all in dire need of new shoes and I couldn't pay the medical bills. I was spread out on the couch, miserably sick from my treatments when my kids rushed through the door from school wearing beautiful new shoes from Laces of Love. We were all so happy! I'll never forget that day. I kept the three Laces of Love shoe tags on my dresser. I've wanted to say thank you for a long time."

Full of gratitude, she poured herself out to me. Her voice began to change and she started to cry. I held her hands in comfort as we stood in a very unlikely place—a shoe aisle in the department store.

Her presence, her struggles and her kind words affirmed the Laces of Love mission. Suddenly I, too, was overcome with emotion.

"Laces of Love helped me and my children during a very difficult time and I thank you so much." She wiped her tears and continued. "I don't know what's going to happen in the future, but today is a good day."

Many high school recipients come back to volunteer for Laces of Love at local events, as J. Destine did, shown here with Jeanne.

Slipping By

High school teacher, Mrs. Dunbar took a deep breath and spoke to me confidentially. "Ana's a tall girl with light brown hair and she shuffles to the back row of my class every day and avoids the other students. Usually, she's a top student, but last week, Ana did poorly on a quiz and failed to turn in her homework. I also noticed that she was wearing musty worn slippers." As Mrs. Dunbar continued her voice became soft. "I was going to approach her but looked into her sad eyes and decided to wait."

Instead, Mrs. Dunbar arranged a meeting with the assistant principal and the guidance counselor. After reviewing her file, Mrs. Dunbar discovered Ana had been cited three times for dress code violations.

The assistant principal spoke up. "Yes, Yes. I remember her. She has been reminded several times about her improper dress code. Wearing slippers is not acceptable. She's been told not to come to school in those slippers again!" He pushed the glasses up on his long nose.

Mrs. Dunbar looked over Ana's file again and said, "She's never been a discipline problem in my class and is a terrific student! I don't see anything else in her file about behavior issues."

The assistant principal reached across the desk and grabbed the file from Mrs. Dunbar's hand. "I warned her of the detentions she'd have and I even slapped the dress code book onto the desk in front of her. Is she choosing to go against our school policy by continuing to wear slippers to school?"

Mrs. Dunbar felt there was more to Ana's story and took the file to the Youth Relations Officer. After reviewing Ana's file, a caseworker was sent to Ana's home—a trailer, located on rental property a mile from the high school. There was not much in the trailer: a beaten up couch, a table, and one wooden chair. There appeared to be nothing that Ana could wear on her feet to school except the slippers. Until this day, no one knew of Ana's home life, full of sadness and despair. No one knew of her troubles, or of the tears that streamed down her cheeks. No one realized her daily concerns about food, shelter, and warm clothes, not just about having only a pair of old discarded slippers to wear to school. After many horrible arguments, the move from one apartment to another and now a decrepit trailer, her family had nothing. Ana carried most of her belongings in an old backpack she had found.

Mrs. Dunbar's concerns were very real and heartbreaking, but she believed that Laces of Love® could help Ana.

A day later, Ana entered the nurse's office feeling broken and confused. She looked up and said, "What's going on? Am I in trouble for the slippers again?" Her voice was soft and her lip quivered in embarrassment.

Mrs. Dunbar quietly closed the door, showed Ana the shoe boxes and explained, "No, Ana, no more troubles with your slippers. These are shoes provided to you by an organization that likes to help good kids like you."

Ana looked up warily. She carefully took the shoes from the boxes and asked, "Two pairs of shoes? Can I keep them both?"

Mrs. Dunbar nodded and watched as Ana pulled the tissue from inside the new shoes.

Ana gasped softly. "These shoes are a miracle." She handled the shoes carefully. "Can I try them on?"

"These two pairs of shoes and socks were especially chosen for you from Laces of Love," Mrs. Dunbar explained.

Ana took off her old slippers and pushed her feet into the new shoes.

Later, Mrs. Dunbar told us, "Watching her sit with the shoes...it was like a great burden had been lifted from her heart and her troubles were now beginning to slip away, just like her old slippers, just slipping away. I never realized that each pair of Laces of Love shoes has a story and in every story, a life is changed."

Piglet noticed that even though he had a Very Small Heart,
it could hold a rather large amount of Gratitude.

~*A.A. Milne*, from *Winnie-the-Pooh*

Dear LACES OF LOVE AND
Dear Dr. Westberry, Last week my
shoes finally broke. They just
fell apart, they had big
holes underneath, the
piece inside my shoe.
Mrs. Lambert had me see
the nurse. She didn't
have a band aide for my
shoes but New shoes.
I wear them everyday.
My Mom was mad at
fist. because she thought
we had to pay, then she
realized they were a gift
forme. My mom and I are
So happy! thank you

The Real Deal

I am often invited to speak to children at local schools. Usually, I'm introduced as "The Shoe Lady" and explain our purpose in giving shoes to needy children. This particular group was full of first and second graders who participated in a donation event for Laces of Love® and each of the children donated one pair of socks if they could. I'm always surprised when I receive unexpected questions and stories from the younger children; they're so spontaneously eager to share.

As I completed my program, many children raised their hands and freely told me their life stories about their shoes. The teachers tried to direct them to only raise their hand if they had a question and one even said, "A question has a question mark at the end of the sentence." She drew a question mark on the whiteboard for all to see.

A teacher noticed Jeremy's hand waving back and forth in the air. "Do you have a question, Jeremy?"

"No, it's not really a real question, but a story." His raspy voice caught my attention.

His teacher politely replied, "Jeremy, we don't have time for stories, so only questions please, for The Shoe Lady."

While the teacher called on other children, Jeremy continued to keep his hand in the air. I answered questions about what kinds of shoes, how many we give, what sizes, and how we count the shoes. Jeremy continued to raise his hand and braced his right arm with his left and started swaying back and forth. He was full of excitement and was so eager to share.

His teacher asked, "Jeremy, do you have a question now?"

"No, I have the real story, the real deal shoes from Laces of Love." The teacher picked another student to ask a question and Jeremy sadly sat back down on the floor.

A small little girl in a soft voice asked, "Um, where do you keep the shoes?"

I explained our process of getting the donations and then filling the orders as coaches, teachers, and shelters requested the shoes of specific sizes.

All at once, Jeremy sprang up from the floor and shouted. "Please can I just tell my story? It's the true life story of the shoes!"

Other children started to snicker and Jeremy turned to his teacher with hope on his face while waiting for her decision.

The teacher looked at him. "Okay, Jeremy."

Jeremy pointed to his shoes. "Hey everybody, look, look right here! These are the real deal. These shoes are real Laces of Love shoes!"

While his classmates and teachers looked at him with disbelief and surprise, he moved near the stage where there was a table.

"Look, I say, look!" Jeremy then hoisted his leg up onto the table and pointed at his shoe. "These are the real deal shoes! Right here, everybody. Just look at them! I had to go to the office yesterday because my shoes were really hurting my feet. My dad told me he couldn't buy me new shoes because we don't have enough money. The guidance counselor said she had some Laces of Love shoes for kids like me. Here they are, the real deal. My brand new shoes from Laces of Love!"

I was asked to be the guest speaker on that day, but the real motivation and excitement was expressed by Jeremy in his new shoes. This was the real deal, just as he proclaimed.

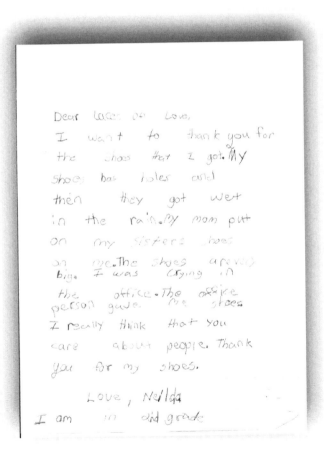

Sole Sistas

"Try outs for the school track team are this Thursday after school," Rosa told Ibbie. Her heart fluttered with excitement. She knew Ibbie was the best runner in the seventh grade.

Looking up from the lunch table, Ibbie said, "I don't know if I can go to the try outs." Her voice was uneasy and she quickly collected her half-eaten apple, sandwich crust, and brushed her crumbs into the brown bag. She hung her head as she left the lunchroom.

"What's wrong with Ibbie?" the other girls asked Rosa.

Rosa frowned and shrugged her shoulders. Rosa and Ibbie had been best friends since they met in third grade. Their families used to share a double-wide trailer in Immokalee. At first the families were disappointed with the living arrangements, but they later discovered that many migrant families shared rooms in the portable trailers. It was a better situation than living in the migrant camps.

Ibbie and Rosa became friends very quickly. They played together and went to school together. Ibbie and Rosa always called themselves Sistas and often chanted, "Same roof over our heads, one wall between our beds!"

Today, Rosa hesitated to approach Ibbie about the tryouts for the middle school track team. Rosa knew Ibbie's family was faced with troubles and her little brother's health issues. She also knew Ibbie could win every single race if she would just come to the tryouts for track. They had talked all summer long about trying out for the track team together.

Now, Ibbie was quiet and sad. She was asked many times to go with her mom to her little brother's doctor appointments to translate the English for her mom so she could understand the medications and treatments. Ibbie didn't mind at first, but now it was difficult because she was missing a lot of school.

After school, Rosa rushed to catch up with Ibbie as she walked home. "Ibbie, why didn't you wait for me?" she asked.

Ibbie continued walking as she answered. "I have to get home. Mom needs me to translate some notes from the doctor's office."

Rosa looked at her friend sincerely. "Ibbie, I really want us to try out for track on Thursday. Please stop and talk to me. Tell me what's the matter. What is it really?" Rosa followed Ibbie down the sidewalk.

"Ibbie, you are my Sista, remember? We talked about tryouts all summer long. It's track season now and you won't even talk about it." Rosa's voice was insistent and troubled.

Ibbie stopped and looked at Rosa. Ibbie wanted to tell her the truth, but she was too embarrassed. It wasn't the time she spent translating for her mom or the chores she had to help with at home, and it wasn't the fact that they still lived in the beat-up trailer with paint chipping inside; no, it was more than all those things.

Suddenly, Ibbie took off running down the street.

"Ibbie, wait! Don't run off! You know I can't catch you!" Rosa yelled. She tossed her book bag over her shoulders and chased after her friend.

The girls continued down the sidewalk passing many other students dragging along after school. Clumps of kids standing in the grass and surrounding neighborhoods watched as the girls raced by.

A young man named Gaspar shouted, "Hey! Are you guys practicing for try-outs already?"

The next day, Ibbie waited outside her trailer for Rosa. Rosa's family had moved into a small house a year ago, which was located one block north of the trailer park. Ibbie was happy for Rosa's family. It was a dream they both shared. This gave Ibbie hope for her family to one day move into a house of their own.

The warm sun beat down on Ibbie's face. When Ibbie saw Rosa coming up the dirt trail by the trailer park, she called, "Hey, Rosa! I guess I can't keep a secret from my Sista!"

Rosa smiled. "Ibbie, please tell me what's going on."

Ibbie motioned Rosa to sit next to her. "Can you keep a secret?"

"For you, of course." Rosa gave her a reassuring look.

"About four weeks ago I lost my shoes. I only had one pair from last year. They were sort of tight on my feet, but I told my mom I could wear them one more year. But I lost them." Ibbie gestured to the shoes on her feet. "I only have these sandals and I don't know what happened to my other shoes. I think someone took them off our trailer steps out front."

Rosa looked down at Ibbie's feet. "Where did those sandals come from?"

"My mom gave me these and she's wearing an old pair of flip-flops."

Rosa noticed the frayed straps and worn leather on her best friend's feet.

Ibbie looked down. "We don't have any extra money right now and I can't ask my mom to buy me anything, especially shoes. I can't try out for the track team without running shoes."

Rosa sat next to Ibbie. It all seemed so hopeless. The fastest runner in seventh grade couldn't even run because she had no shoes?

They both had worn second-hand clothes and shoes over the years and shared sweaters and jackets. When their church gave away free socks last Christmas, it was a gift of luxury. Now what?

Ibbie sighed, dropped her head and fiddled with the old straps on her sandals. "All of our dreams are crushed. Now we can't compete in the middle school track meets together."

Then, Rosa jumped up. "It's not hopeless, Ibbie. I have a plan!"

"What are you talking about?"

Rosa talked rapidly. "I have this pair of size 6 running shoes and I know you wear size 7, but can you squeeze your foot into them?"

"What are you talking about? Why?"

"Ibbie, we can share the shoes!"

"What? You mean we both wear your shoes? How?"

"We race different races, right? I run long distance and you are the greatest sprinter. We'll just run our different races and share the shoes. It'll be our secret."

Suddenly, Ibbie understood. "That's a great idea, but we have to keep it a secret." She shook her head. "I don't want anyone to know."

Rosa smiled. "Our secret, Sista! We'll share my shoes and no one will know. We'll still be Sistas; sole sisters, like our shoes!"

They started to giggle and realized they were going to be late for school.

Slipping off her old sandals, Ibbie jabbed Rosa in the side and said, "Race you to school!" She took off barefoot down the street.

Rosa yelled after her, "You run fast, even barefoot!"

* * *

Thursday's try-outs for track went as planned. Rosa wore the size 6 running shoes for the first try-out and placed third in the two-mile race. She made the track team.

Then, Rosa met Ibbie behind the building and they exchanged shoes. Ibbie pushed her larger foot into the size 6 blue shoes and smiled at Rosa. She was so grateful for her Sole Sista. Ibbie had a terrific race, coming in first out of ten girls. Ibbie and Rosa jumped around on the track together when their coach said, "Both of you should be very proud of yourselves. Not many seventh graders make the middle school team!"

Ibbie felt her feet starting to swell inside the smaller running shoes, but she didn't dare say a word to Coach or to her best friend.

The coach posted the team races every practice and Rosa's grand idea to share the shoes was working fine. Rosa would run the two-mile and other long distance races, then Ibbie would wear the shoes for her sprints and the shorter races.

No one knew their secret—or the pain that Ibbie felt. Her feet often swelled up after practice and blisters started to form on her toes. Her heels were also bothering her, but she decided to never say a word about the pain, not even to Rosa, because this was a tremendous gift and she was so grateful.

Competing in different races and heats allowed the girls to keep their secret. The coach was pleased with their times on the track and encouraged them both to continue practicing before the first competition against other middle schools.

After a few weeks of track practice, the day had finally arrived for the very first middle school track meet. Ibbie and Rosa huddled together in the locker room looking over their new red and white uniforms.

Rosa's long distance race was the first of the track meet. Ibbie stood on the sidelines coaching her in the warm ups, "Come on, Sista, you can do this! You can win this race. Make it yours."

Rosa looked over at Ibbie, and grinned. Suddenly, the starting gun sounded and the girls were off. It was a long race and Ibbie never took her eyes off her friend. Rosa was thrilled to place third out of twelve girls. Rushing to the side of the building, the girls exchanged shoes and Ibbie scrambled to get onto the track for her upcoming race.

The starting gun sounded and Ibbie took off. She curled the turns easily, gaining speed and passing all the other sprinters. The excitement of the crowd cheering her on helped eliminate the pain in her feet. The shoes were so tight for her feet. Although she could feel the swelling, she would keep the secret.

After Ibbie won the race, the announcer yelled, "And that, Ladies and Gentleman, was amazing! That young seventh grader just set a record for this track!" The fans jumped up and down and cheered. Ibbie dashed off to the middle of the field to celebrate with Rosa.

The two girls fell into each other's arms and danced around the field. All their teammates ran out to the field and surrounded them, jumping up and down and chanting, "Ib-bie! Ib-bie! Ib-bie!"

At that moment, the coach happened to look down and noticed Rosa in her bare feet and Ibbie wearing the familiar blue shoes; the same blue shoes that Rosa had worn at practice and in today's meet.

He was stunned. The two girls were sharing the same pair of shoes—shoes that were too small for one of the best runners on his team. Imagine how she'd do if she had shoes that fit!

The very next morning, the coach contacted Laces of Love® and two pairs of new running shoes were delivered to the school that day. Coach called the girls into his office. "I know what you've been doing, and I know your secret," he said kindly.

Ibbie and Rosa looked at each other in disbelief. Coach looked down at Ibbie's sore feet and her worn sandals. Her feet were full of blisters. She tucked her feet under the chair out of sight.

The coach smiled. "Ibbie, the shoes are too small for your feet so Laces of Love donated a new pair just your size. I told them about you girls sharing one pair of shoes. They heard your story and donated another pair for Rosa, too, because of her love and kindness."

The girls just looked at each other then back to Coach. "You both have a new pair of running shoes from Laces of Love! Now, try not to mix up the sizes because they are the exact same shoes." He looked at Ibbie. "But they will fit your feet!"

The girls were so excited they jumped from their seats and hugged their coach. They tried the shoes on and hugged him again. The coach later called Laces of Love and said, "I felt guilty getting the hugs and receiving all the joy from giving the shoes. It was Laces of Love that deserved the hugs and the smiles from Ibbie and Rosa, the Sole Sistas!"

5/24/10

I want to Thank laces of Love for giving me the Sneakers. My DAD is in Jail and My MoM is trying her best to make ends meet. So this will help her so much.

Thank You
Christian

EAST NAPLES MIDDLE SCHOOL
4100 Estey Avenue ~ Naples, Florida 34104

Shoes for Sale

Rushing from one school to the next, I had a hectic day. The last thing I wanted to do was go out that Monday evening. As I drove into the garage, I noticed my husband dashing from the house to greet me.

"Hurry, we're running late. Get ready and I'll be in the car!"

I could hear the urgency in his voice. We were to pick up another couple on the way to our Monday night engagement.

He was so excited about attending this event at the local college. It was called "Night of the Nest," a fund-raiser for the athletics of Florida Gulf Coast University (FGCU). Recently the university had become well known for advancing into the basketball tournament and had earned the title, "Dunk City."

As I changed my clothes, I heard the car horn sound in quick succession. "Okay, Okay, I'm coming!" I said to myself as I grabbed my bag and shoes and darted out the door.

"You're always on time. What's up?" Donald asked as I got into the car.

"Sorry," I said. "I had a crazy day. I delivered to six different schools all over the place in the pouring rain and the traffic was awful." I continued complaining as I searched my purse for some lipstick.

Looking at his watch, he said, "All right. We'll make it on time." He took a deep breath of relief. "We'll pick up Bill and his wife and be at the college in 20 minutes."

Pulling the passenger mirror down, I flipped it over and regretted looking. I had hair flying everywhere and my eyes were bloodshot. After dabbing the pink lipstick onto my lips, I added a dot to each cheek, rubbing it all together like soft sunburn. I was good to go.

When we reached the university, the parking lot was full, so we jetted into a side lot and rushed to get inside. There were booths, tables, raffles, and waiters serving drinks at high top tables. The decorated gymnasium was full of spirited fans. Blue and green streamers fluttered from the rafters and the Eagle Mascot circulated the room.

The event featured several speakers: the president of the college, the basketball coach and many others, but it was the young man who stood like a giant on the stage who caught my interest. He spoke about his college days and the influence of his coach and terrific team that helped get him where he is today, playing for the Chicago White Sox. He was a pitcher in the Major Leagues! At 6-foot-6, he stood at the podium in blazer, jeans, and brown boots. Chris Sale spoke words of appreciation. He spoke with sincerity as he expressed his gratitude, and I was touched by his humble words.

Turning to my husband I said, "He pitches in the majors?"

My husband nodded. "Yes."

"He's a great guy!" I said.

Smiling, my husband said, "He's a great baseball player!"

As I watched him with his wife, Brianne, and his small son, Rylan, I thought, Now that is the kind of person I wish I could speak with to help Laces of Love®.

While walking out of the event that night, I felt blessed to have heard such an amazing athlete share his story and thank his fans, his college team, and the community that supported him in his early years.

As the baseball season continued that year, I often heard my husband say, "Jeanne, come here. Chris Sale is on television again. He broke another record! He is a terrific pitcher."

And other times, Chris Sale was featured on the sports page for another win, another strike out, another victory for the 6-foot-6 player from FGCU. I collected a few articles and saved his picture. I said a few prayers for him and his career. I had a special place saved in my heart for this pro baseball player who smiled and was generous to his fans.

Move forward one year later. It's early autumn.

Running from the garage to the kitchen with two bags full of new shoes in my arms, I fumbled to get to the answering machine.

"Hello, my name is Brianne Sale and I'm very interested in learning more about your charity, Laces of Love. Please give me a call back as soon as you can."

This message was one of five messages that I received that morning. Two were from Lee County school nurses who left messages earlier requesting shoes for needy kids. One message was from a Collier County football coach needing cleats for a few of his players and another message was a reminder that I was speaking to the Girl Scouts on Saturday. I sat at my desk to record the numbers then sighed and slipped off my shoes.

Growing up, my mom taught me many things and one was to always return your phone calls. So I started with the school nurses that day and ended with the sweet woman named Brianne Sale.

She told me she was enrolled at Florida Gulf Coast University and she was to get involved with a local non-for profit and learn how it operates. She said, "I decided I want to get more involved and would like to volunteer. My husband would like to help, too."

Out of all the phone calls that morning, this was the first voice offering to help me with Laces of Love, instead of asking me for something. I was curious to hear more. Pouring a cup of coffee and grabbing a note pad, I was prepared to listen.

Brianne Sale continued, "I'm taking a class at Florida Gulf Coast University and I want to get more involved in the community and learn about your charity. My husband likes your charity because you give new sneakers and also new athletic shoes. You might know my husband. His name is Chris Sale and he plays for the Chicago White Sox."

As she spoke, I frantically took notes, writing as fast as I could to record all the information into my Laces notebook. When she said the name Chris Sale, I jotted it down and then suddenly, I stopped.

"Brianne, you mean Chris Sale from FGCU baseball?" I asked intently.

"Yes. He plays for the White Sox now. Do you know who he is?" she politely asked.

"Yes, I think so! I was at 'Night in the Nest' and heard him speak last year." I continued to listen with anticipation growing inside me.

Brianne calmly explained her college course and the expectations she wanted to meet. She said she had contacted two other local charities but had not heard back from them. She thanked me for returning her phone call and said she wanted to meet in person and discuss how she and Chris could help Laces of Love. We discussed the charity and our mission and many other things that day. Then we set a date for a breakfast meeting and Brianne invited my husband, too.

When we hung up, I sat for a moment in disbelief. I pulled out a box of programs from the past basketball season at FGCU and the program for "Night of the Nest." I looked at the photo of Chris Sale and thought, Boy, is my husband going to be excited about this fund-raiser!

The Saturday of the breakfast meeting, my husband and I arrived 20 minutes early. We were both excited and felt blessed that someone was taking interest in our little charity. While waiting for Brianne and Chris to arrive, we sipped hot coffee at a round table on the restaurant patio. It was a beautiful cool morning and we treasured our moment together.

Laces of Love is a charity that has tied us to many wonderful children and families. Now God was blessing us with this new opportunity, having breakfast with Brianne and Chris Sale.

Not knowing what to expect, we eagerly watched each car that pulled into the parking lot. A brilliant red corvette quickly slid into a space, then a black convertible BMW circulated the parking lot.

"That's not them, Jeanne." My husband identified the car models and the probable owners. Out of the corner of my eye, I saw a large white truck easing into a spot in front of the patio. The wheels were big and jacked up about 5 feet off the pavement. Out stepped the tall young man with the confident grin and his beautiful wife. Brianne had kind eyes and a warm inviting smile as she reached for my hand. Chris towered over us in his t-shirt, jeans, and brown boots. He stretched his arm down to shake our hands, and I watched as my husband glowed in the moment.

Brianne and Chris were so wonderful to meet in person. They were excited to learn about Laces and how they could help. Little did I know, this was the beginning of a partnership and also a new wonderful friendship.

I shared many stories about children who needed shoes and the beginnings of the Laces of Love Charitable Foundation years ago in my home. Chris listened and Brianne asked questions. They looked through my scrapbook full of many pictures of kids in new shoes. After our first breakfast meeting, Chris and Brianne said they wanted to help Laces of Love by hosting an event at FGCU.

Within a few days, the FGCU Athletic Department contacted me and set up a meeting. Within a few weeks, I met Chris and Brianne Sale in the lobby of Alico Arena. Amazingly, we were going in to present our charity to staff members of Florida Gulf Coast University. I was prepared to give my speech and try to persuade members of the Athletic Department to host a Laces of Love Night at FGCU.

After polite introductions, I began to discuss Laces of Love and our mission. While sharing stories about children in need, I was suddenly interrupted by Chris. He pulled his leather chair closer to the conference table, adjusted his long legs, and started to talk. He talked and talked and talked as he described every child that I had told him about needing shoes. His voice was strong and he tapped his boots under the table as he spoke.

He retold every story that I had shared with him. Stories about little children who had to wear last year's old shoes to school, shoes too small for their growing feet. Chris asked for a Laces of Love Night—at Alico Arena. His wife smiled as she gently kicked my foot under the table.

Brianne whispered, "Jeanne, he thinks he's on your board." She was a bit shocked at his eagerness to push through the mission and discuss the kids and their needs. She watched and smiled as he continued to talk and talk about Laces of Love.

I felt my heart pounding as I listened and watched Chris. It was so exciting to hear him talking about our charity, and everyone in that room really started to listen. They looked at Chris and recognized his passion for children who couldn't afford a pair of shoes. His words were full of emotion as he reached for my scrapbook. He looked at me and said, "I want to help Jeanne and her mission to put shoes on kids in need. I want to help her in a big way."

Emotions flooded his face as his voice started to crack a little. "I can't imagine a high school baseball player having the desire to play ball and not having the proper shoes or baseball cleats to compete. It's just not right." Shaking his head and looking down, he continued. "We need to help. Brianne and I really want to help."

All eyes in that room were focused on Chris.

"Chris," the Athletic Director asked, "what do you and Brianne have in mind?"

"Let's have a basketball game and host a Laces of Love Shoe Drive!"

Within a few minutes, the date was set, a flyer was drafted, and FGCU was on board.

I wanted to jump from my seat and shout the FGCU Fight Song. I wanted to reach up and wrap my arms around both of the Sales. Brianne's eyes were bright and her smile stretched across the room. Everyone was smiling and Chris sat tall looking over at me. He winked at Brianne and then tapped the scrapbook with his long fingers. The hands that toss the best pitch in town, the hands that lead him to the major leagues had just pitched our mission of Laces of Love and it was a home run.

As we walked down the halls of the Athletic Department, located behind the scenes at Alico Arena, I noticed for the first time the decorated posters, jerseys, and pictures of All Star, Chris Sale.

For a few years now, Chris and Brianne have promoted Laces of Love and made donations of new shoes and athletic shoes. Florida Gulf Coast University has hosted a Chris and Brianne Sale/Laces of Love Night and raised money and collected new shoes for needy children. They are true Shoe Angels! Their son Rylan helps collect and tag the shoes that are donated. It is a family affair at Dunk City!

At the Florida Gulf Coast University Shoe Drive for Laces of Love. Left to right: Laces of Love Board Member, Geralyn Krout; FGCU Mascot Eagle; Co-founder, Jeanne Nealon; Chris, Brianne, and Rylan Sale.

"It is only with the heart that one can see rightly; what is essential is invisible to the eye."

~Antoine de Saint-Exupéry,
from *The Little Prince*

Eli and Two Different Shoes

Laces of Love® is invited to participate in many outreach programs throughout the year to help provide new shoes to many other not-for-profit children's organizations. In August, we were invited to participate in a large, community outreach Back-to-School event.

All of our volunteers arrived early to set up and organize the new shoes. We'd measure children's feet with special foot-sizing devices and fit them with the correct size as other groups gave out school supplies and backpacks. It was great fun watching the kids get their new shoes and then give the volunteers high fives, hugs, and big smiles.

Hundreds of children lined up with their families for this event. The lines were long and they waited patiently, sitting on little elementary chairs without complaining. In the midst of the chaos and the shuffling of children, I noticed a tall, lanky kid in tattered jeans and a frayed hoodie who flopped down in the little chair with two different shoes on his feet.

"I'm starting a trend," he said and I smiled, noticing that the shoes are obviously two different sizes. "Okay, not really starting a trend," he admitted. He looked at me and shrugged; his blue eyes warmed my heart.

When his feet got measured, the actual size was much bigger than both of the shoes he was wearing. He hung his head low and swallowed. I was baffled; not only did he have two different shoes on his feet, they were two different sizes! The room was buzzing with noise and chatter, but suddenly I was lost in the moment. I felt as if the room was standing still.

Voices swirled around my head but I could only see and hear this boy. Sitting with his long legs in the tiny chair, his knees situated under his chin, he looked at me with those gentle blue eyes.

"Come with me," I said and took him to the shoes storage area behind the volunteers and waiting families.

"Am I allowed to go back here? Can you do this?" he asked.

I smiled. "Yeah, I can! Pick any pair of shoes you want from this size area."

He hesitated, embarrassed, but finally made a selection and tried on the shoes. His hands shook and tears glistened on his face. I handed him another name-brand pair of shoes to put in his new backpack. Tearfully, he told me he lived at Youth Haven and his dad lived at the shelter, St. Matthews House. He explained that they moved here to start a new life.

He shook my hand and his gentle blue eyes conveyed his appreciation. He turned to walk away into the crowd. Then, in that moment, he looked back and waved to me. I will never forget that blue-eyed, gentle young man who had two different shoes before this day and now faced the next day with hope.

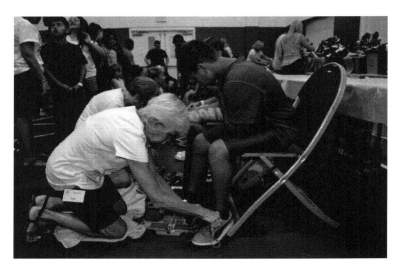

Friends of Foster Care event. Volunteers measuring children's feet to find the perfect fit.

Footwork

After speaking to a group of teachers and administrators, I was approached by a man who tapped me on the shoulder and said, "I would really like to speak with you, Jeanne, please."

I was surrounded by teachers and administrators asking for my card and Laces of Love® brochures, but the troubled look on his face and his anxiety expressed an urgency. Placing brochures onto the podium for others to take, I quickly followed the nervous man into the hallway. I noticed the whistle on a lanyard draped around his thick neck and his tight coaching shirt exposing his lean body.

"I'm the head high school football coach and, well, you said that these kids who need shoes for school also need football and soccer cleats and you know, good athletic shoes. Well, I know this kid, this football player on my team..."

Nodding, I listened intently. The whistle moved back and forth on his chest as he talked, and his face began to change color as beads of sweat bubbled up on his forehead. The coach stopped, looked down at this hands and tried to continue, but there was a quiver in his voice.

Sensing his nervousness, I tried to help him. "Yes, I can help. Here's my card. Call me, call Laces of Love and we'll get you shoes, athletic shoes, or whatever you—"

He interrupted firmly. "No, Jeanne, no. I have to tell you something. You see, I have this kid, a player on my team and I knew something was wrong all season long and I did nothing. He's a big player, over two hundred pounds, and plays on the offensive line." The coach paused, looked down and tried to hide the tears in his eyes. "He sits on the bench in the locker room and waits until everyone is out on the field and then asks me for my athletic tape."

The coach rubbed his thick hands together. "He asks me every day. This kid sits there as I grab my clipboard and fumble through my papers of drills and plays. I look over and he waits patiently and quietly on the locker room bench. Waiting for me, the head coach who doesn't know."

Despite his emotion, he's determined to tell me his story. "He wants to borrow the tape we use to wrap the ankles of our quarterback and our top running back. The tape provides tightness and support for their ankles. But this young man wants to borrow my tape." He rubbed the back of his neck. "I was annoyed. I don't want to give him more tape. He's using up all the good tape; it's supposed to be for my top players. I would become so irritated with this big kid. But after hearing you speak about shoes and kids in need...I suddenly realized something."

He wiped away the tears on his cheeks. "He was asking for my tape, because he was taping his shoes together; he was taping his football cleats. He comes from a family of five children. His dad lost his job and they are struggling financially. I couldn't see what was right in front of me; he was using the tape for his old cleats. I didn't see the truth under my nose."

We both cried and I reached out and hugged him. With the pure simplicity of this discovery, he was moved to action.

"Please, let me help," I said. "Laces of Love can provide him with football cleats and new shoes today. What's his size?"

"No, Jeanne," he said with a big sigh. "No, I want to buy him new football cleats and new school shoes. I want to do the footwork."

His genuine sincerity and words would carry him to seasons of giving. I can still see him smiling with determination to make a difference. Amazingly, this coach has continued to purchase shoes for Laces of Love and has helped give to other athletes in need for many years. When my mother passed away, he dropped off a box of new soccer and football cleats to my doorstep in honor of my mom, who knew his story.

He also continues to stock athletic tape on his locker room shelves for any athletes that needs to tape up their shoulders, arms, or ankles, but not shoes. He'll provide the shoes by doing the footwork.

East Lee High School basketball players in Lehigh Acres (Lee County) are delighted to have court shoes that fit properly. Emmanuel (left) and Joseph (right) are pictured here with Jeanne.

Letters of Love

Dear Laces of Love,

I just wanted to say thank you for the new shoes. I really appreciate it. This year has been very hard on my family considering my dad was laid off from his job. Laces of Love has given our family new shoes for a couple of years now and it has helped so much. Our family can worry about other things.

I was thinking, this year, since I have a job now, instead of receiving shoes, I would like to buy shoes for kids just like me. A pair of new tennis shoes for school is something most people take for granted, but I know a pair of shoes means so much more. A new pair of shoes can help a child have more confidence and feel better about themselves at school. Laces of Love has made a difference in my life, and I want to help other kids! Thank you for helping my family over the years.

Sincerely,
Kailee, a high school graduate

Dear Laces of Love,

As a teacher, I see many needs. I will never forget the first pair of new shoes I was able to pass on to a third grader in my class. I'll call him, Frankie.

Frankie was small, had wild curly hair and had many needs. He often came to school in clothes that smelled dirty, had no school supplies or lunch money. During recess he sometimes ran out of his shoes, which were much too big for him. It was obvious that his heart screamed out, "Pick me, pick me!" for the games, but he often lagged behind the other kids on the playground, just struggling to walk in his old, floppy shoes.

Thanks to Laces of Love, we were able to give him a brand new pair of tennis shoes in the privacy of the school nurse's office. You would have thought he had won the lottery; the biggest smile I have ever seen spread across his face!

In his excitement, he burst back through the classroom doors and said, "Look everyone! Look!" Frankie pointed to his shoes. "I have good shoes and I am just like you!"

The other children broke out into a wild applause! It was a major first step for Frankie and I believe he grew a couple of inches in that very moment. Thank you for boosting his self-esteem in a third grade moment I am sure he and his classmates will never forget.

Frankie's Third Grade Teacher

Dear Jeanne,

I wish everyone understood how important Laces of Love is to these kids in Immokalee. Most of these families work in the field and are struggling to get by let alone buy a new pair of shoes for their children. Some are students living with their grandparents who just can't afford to buy them shoes.

The smile on a child's face when we give them new shoes is priceless, especially when they are wearing an old pair too big or too small.

One little girl said, "I am so happy today. I have a new pair of shoes and my birthday was yesterday."

Later, I found out that was her only birthday present.

**Migrant Resource Teacher
in Collier County Schools**

Dear Laces of Love,

Believe me, we thank you mentally all the time, but I wanted to share with you two incidents that happened yesterday with our students and your shoes.

The first young boy came to my office and asked if we had any shoes that would fit him. He was wearing shoes that were so tight he could hardly walk. We found him a pair that fit and when he tried them on, breathed a sigh of relief and headed back to class.

The second incident involved a third grade girl. I was visiting her classroom and found her despondent and uncommunicative. I knew her mother was going through chemotherapy, so I pulled her into an adjoining room and checked to see how she was doing. She had on a huge pair of tennis shoes, a size 6. She was upset because other children were teasing her about the big shoes she had to wear. A friend of her mother's gave them to her and she had to wear them because her old shoes were too small and hurt her feet. I found her a pair of size 2 pink shoes and she hugged me and cried with relief. Your efforts touch children every day and we thank you so much.

A Principal in Collier County

Dear Laces of Love,

I first heard about Laces of Love in 2006 from a teacher that had heard about you providing shoes to needy students. I looked you up on the Internet and came across your website. I took down the telephone number to President, Jeanne Nealon and gave her a call. Talking to her was like talking to a friend I'd known all my life. We clicked instantly!

Jeanne was the nicest lady I had met. I feel God had this plan for us to meet so we could help needy students together. I explained to her about the situation with our migrant students in Immokalee Middle School and how many of them live in sub-standard conditions and their parents struggle just to provide the basics, such as food, shelter and clothing. Their parents work extreme hours, like from 6 a.m. to dark. Older siblings have to fend for themselves and their younger brothers and sisters. Right away she sent the first Laces of Love donation of 32 pairs of shoes. It was awesome! The students that received those shoes were ecstatic.

Since then, Laces of Love has provided about 160 pairs of shoes and any special requests I have in between, are also filled. In addition, Laces of Love has provided shoes for our Boys and Girls Program in Immokalee, supplied cleats for our soccer team and provided running shoes for our cross-country students.

Hopefully she won't be upset that I mention the following. I will never forget one time several years ago that I really needed shoes for our students. Jeanne wasn't sure if Laces had the funds to get shoes for us, so she asked her husband, "as an anniversary gift," to take her to Sports Authority, and they bought about 100 pairs of brand new shoes for us. Of course that sweet man agreed and we got our shoes! Jeanne did not mention this story to me until the shoes were distributed.

The impact those shoes make on our students is amazing. A lot of these students were just coming from Mexico and Haiti and can't afford clothes or food, let alone shoes. Here are some of the things students have said to me when they receive new shoes:

"These are the very first shoes I have that are new!"

"How much do I owe you? (not knowing they were free).

"I feel so tall!"

I've seen students wear their Dad's shoes, their brother's smaller shoes, high heels and flip flops, just because they didn't have anything else to wear. Some kids asked me for glue to hold their shoes together, and one girl gave the brand-new shoes she received to her older pregnant sister because her feet were aching (She received another pair for her sister and was so happy!)

To be honest, I don't know what I'd do without the kindness of this group. I'm honored to know Laces of Love because they truly care about our students as if they were their own.

Migrant Resource Teacher
Immokalee Middle School

New Horizons Super Kids Club. From left to right: Co-founder Jeanne Nara Nealon; student, Jose Cisuenpes; Co-founders Susan Warren and Mary Nara Myrmo.

Oneliz Cruz smiling as she ties her new Laces of Love shoes.

Call to Action

You can help in **many** ways

Shoe Angels (above) and (below) Board Members serving as greeters at "From Jazz to Broadway" annual fundraiser. It's the volunteers who help make Laces of Love events happen.

Lacing a Strong Relationship

- When a child can't take a physical education class because she only has a pair of flip-flops to wear

- When a second-grader is sitting on the bench in front of the school and crying, holding her broken sandal

- When they need shoes for their track and cross-country teams

- When a football player only has a pair of cleats that are so small they raise daily blisters

- When a child is too embarrassed to come to school in his dad's old shoes

- When two girls share one pair of shoes on the high school track team

- When a teacher finds a child hiding in a restroom because kids are teasing her about her smelly shoes

- When a group of teachers wants to provide shoes with VELCRO® fasteners for their special needs students

They turn to Laces of Love® for understanding, support, and new shoes.

Ten Reasons to Participate with Laces of Love®

1. Buying shoes is great fun and one pair of shoes truly makes a difference.
2. Gifting a child with a new pair of shoes raises self-esteem and confidence.
3. Donating new shoes to aspiring athletes can give them a confidence edge.
4. Telling others about Laces of Love® spreads kindness and love.
5. Providing a child with his first pair of new shoes creates a magical moment.
6. Experiencing the gratification from helping a child is immeasurable.
7. Donating gives you the opportunity to help children in your own community.
8. Giving shoes to needy children enables their caregivers to focus on health and nutrition.
9. Providing much-needed comfort to deserving children without resources.
10. Inspiring the recipients of these shoes to pay it forward some day as adults.

We make a living by what we get.
We make a life by what we give.
~Winston Churchill

Delivering Back-to-School shoes for needy kids in Lee
County: Hope Cliff, Jill Koisa, Jeanne, and Hannah Cliff.

People will forget what you said,
people may forget what you did, but they will
never forget how you made them feel.
~Maya Angelou

Shoe donations loaded up after a recent Shoe Party.

Many classrooms host fundraisers and collect shoes. Royal Palm Academy student Dexter Clark, tells Jeanne, "Big shoes to fill! I wonder how big this boy is who will get these shoes!"

How to Host a Laces of Love® Event
(It's super easy and lots of fun for everyone!)

Gather some of your favorite people from your community association, alumnae group, golfing buddies, tennis team, church group, sorority, bridge club, colleagues, soccer moms, bowling league, your kids and their in-laws, neighbors, relatives, or good friends and invite them for brunch, lunch, tea, dinner, cocktails, BBQ, dessert, your birthday, the holidays, or a beach party.

- Ask them to bring one (or more) pairs of *new* sneakers for a needy child. *All* sizes are needed—especially boys and girls sizes 1-6.
- Shoes will be tagged with a Laces of Love® tag and distributed through the public schools and/or organizations that serve needy children in Collier and Lee counties. Give your guests a really good time *and* introduce them to Laces of Love.
- Encourage your guests to give a Laces Shoe Party or to make a monetary donation to: Laces of Love Charitable Foundation, 1976 Bethany Place, Naples, FL 34109. One hundred percent of monetary donations are used to purchase new shoes for needy kids. Laces of Love is **100 percent** volunteers.
- Call Jeanne (239)-591-1172 for information or to arrange a local pick up of the shoes your group collected for our students.

How to Start a Laces of Love®-type Charity

1. **Be open to what your name might be.** Test ideas on Google search and with your state's and the IRS list of non-profits—to be sure the name you are considering is available. For example, Laces of Love® is Service Marked, which means no one can use that name without our permission. Play around with possibilities for your name, colors, logo, etc. Choose a name that is specific for your charity and mission! Do not take someone else's mission or idea or name!

2. **Decide what kind(s) of shoes you will collect and donate.**

   Hint: if you decide to collect "gently used shoes," you *will* get a fair number of totally worn out shoes—old, smelly, disgusting. Remember, many economically disadvantaged kids have never had a pair of new shoes. To Laces, *new* shoes are the shoes you will want.

   "Party" or "Sunday" shoes are nice—but kids *need* sneakers. Without sneakers, they can't take PE or run or play the way kids should. Define the type of shoes that are right for you.

3. **Decide how you will get your shoes to your "clients."** And how and who will decide who should receive the shoes.

   Laces of Love relies on school counselors, school nurses, teachers, administrators or program directors and other staff from non-profits who serve "Laces" kids to determine who needs shoes. We do not make that decision.

Laces of Love decided early on to serve kids, age birth through 18. We do not serve adults.

We look closely every year at the school districts' data about the number of kids receiving free lunches. That gives us a good idea of the overall need even though every child on free lunches does not need shoes.

We also have learned that need is everywhere. Several years ago, a high school band from a well-to-do high school held a shoe drive for Laces of Love. We got a call from the mom of one of the students who explained she simply couldn't provide a pair of new shoes for the drive—her own daughter was squeezing into last year's shoes. (We got a new pair of shoes to the daughter plus a pair for the shoe drive.)

We try hard to meet the need but not be taken advantage of. Shoes are given in the privacy of school/non-profit offices. Shoes have been taken out of the shoeboxes (it's possible to store more shoes on the "shoe closet" shelf at school) and have a Laces of Love tag attached to them so the child can show his or her parents where the shoes came from, but we leave it up to the child to disclose that he or she has received "Laces" shoes.

We deliver 25-100 pairs of shoes of various, appropriate sizes to every school in Collier and Lee counties (Florida) a few days before the first day of school. Once those shoes (or the shoes in a popular size) are given out, the point person at the school (school nurse, counselor, etc.) will call us with requests for individual kids they have identified as needing shoes. They measure the child's foot. We add one size to the current foot size and deliver a pair of shoes to the school for that child. If possible, we include one pair of new socks.

When we deliver shoes to a school, we have the school recipient (this could be the school secretary) sign a sheet noting how many shoes were delivered. We later tally these "Distribution Sheets" to tell how many shoes were distributed annually to a particular school, the school district (county), and overall.

We are aware of styles and colors that are more popular and try to select shoes the child will like and be proud to wear, but we do not let the child request a specific brand or a specific color. We will deliver VELCRO®-closing shoes to special needs kids, if requested.

4. **Advisors and Volunteers.** We have a small group of board members and special volunteers that we entrust with delivering shoes. Shoe delivery people must be willing to drive their own cars over a large geographic area, must have valid drivers licenses, and auto insurance. (We know them personally and trust them with thousands of dollars worth of shoes for a large delivery.)

5. **Decide how you will gather shoes to distribute.** The easiest way to start is to have Shoe Parties (see notes about How to Have a Shoe Party). Encourage supporters to have their own shoe parties or to have guests bring a pair of new shoes to a dinner party in lieu of a hostess gift.

Be prepared: people love donating the cute, little kid shoes. People think kids have small feet. You will have to work to educate folk that kids' feet are large!

Thank everyone who gives you anything. A personal (handwritten) note is lovely.

6. **Dealing with Donations.** If you are going to accept monetary donations, you should explore incorporating and applying for 501-c-3 status with the IRS. Find an attorney to help with the incorporation process (pro bono, of course) and a CPA to help with your 501-c-3 application (ditto).

   You will need to file a Form 990 (or 990-EZ) with the IRS. You can request an extension every year for the filing date—thus allowing your CPA to complete the 990 in the summer, when he or she is not that busy.

7. **If you are buying shoes, look for sales!** The Laces of Love buyers are *the* best at finding terrific shoe sales. Laces has a small business VISA card which we use for all purchases. Early on, board members made a purchase, paid personally, and were reimbursed when they turned their receipt in to the treasurer. No receipt—no reimbursement.

8. **A word about brochures and PR**. Everyone wants to see photos of kids with their new shoes. BUT, you cannot publish a photo of a child under 18 (even on Facebook) unless a parent or guardian has signed a waiver.

   Use the tried and true: Who, what, where, when, why, and how when you write any copy for brochures, press releases, web pages, etc.

9. **Start small.** The first year of Laces, we gave out 23 pairs of shoes. The second year, we outfitted 65 needy kids at very "at risk" schools with new shoes. By 2015, 9, 912 kids in Collier and Lee counties received shoes from Laces of Love.

Only do what you can do. Remember that the kids you serve probably would not be wearing such nice, new shoes, that fit properly, if it weren't for you.

Celebrate often and have fun!

Shoe drive at a local arena filled the bed of this pick-up truck with new shoes.

A Note from the Author

This book would not be possible without the input of many people including my editors Jory Westberry and Lisa Wroble, and of course the Laces of Love® Board of Directors and my Co-founders.

As I wrote this book, I realized that all through my life many people had a tremendously positive influence on guiding me on this journey. My loving parents, my sisters and brothers, my husband and my sons have all provided me with support and love and taught me that the true meaning of love is in giving. From the sisters at Notre Dame College of Ohio, to the wonderful volunteers on my board of directors since the beginning of Laces of Love—all have contributed to the gift of a pair of shoes. Ever since my confirmation day, I have cherished and admired my little Saint Bernadette. She was a poor child who called herself a humble servant. She continues to teach me about showing a little kindness each day and that this simple act brings so much joy to others.

The most important light in my life is my Savior, Jesus Christ. I dedicate this book and my service of Laces of Love Charitable Foundation, Inc. to Him. His love and grace are enough for me, and I have always tried to surrender it all to be guided by His will. He has brought into my life the wonderful volunteers who help get shoes ready for delivery to schools, work at fundraising benefits, spread the word about our organization, share photos and the wonderful thank you notes from the children we serve, and have helped make this book possible.

(Photo above) Very happy recipients Matthew, Deon, Andy, and Cleo with Jeanne. (Photo below) The Nealon family at a Laces of Love Christmas event: Don, Jeanne, Bryce, and Luke.

Source list
for quotations used throughout this book

Servant Song on secondary title page: From the hymn *Ubi-Caritas* (plainsong) Words: Latin; tr. Joyce MacDonald Glover (b. 1923) Music: *Ubi caritas,* plainsong, Mode 6 <http://www.dragonvet.com/html/hymns/hymn606.htm>

St. Teresa of Calcutta (Mother Teresa) on Dedication page: Catholic Online.<http://www.catholic.org/clife/teresa/quotes.php>

Willa Cather on page 2: Guideposts.org <https://www.guideposts.org/where-there-great-love-there-are-always-miracles>

Pope Francis on page 4: Holy Mass and Canonization of Blessed Mother Teresa of Calcutta, Homily of His Holiness Pope Francis, Saint Peter's Square, September 4, 2016. <https://w2.vatican.va/content/francesco/en/homilies/2016/documents/papa-francesco_20160904_omelia-canonizzazione-madre-teresa.html>

A.A. Milne (from *Winnie-the-Pooh*) on page 7: Goodreads Quotable Quote: A.A. Milne <http://www.goodreads.com/author/show/81466.A_A_Milne>

Robert Fulghum on page 8: in *All I Really Need to Know I Learned in Kindergarten: Uncommon Thoughts on Common Things* by Robert Fulghum. (Ballantine Books; 15th Anniversary edition, 2004)

St. Teresa of Calcutta on page 22: quoted at Dorothy Day Center for Faith & Justice blog, December 19, 2013. <https://dorothydaycfj.wordpress.com/2013/12/19/its-not-how-much-we-give-but-how-much-love-we-put-into-giving/>

Robert H. Schuller on page 41: quoted in Chapter 4 of *A Book of Miracles: Inspiring True Stories of Healing, Gratitude, and Love* by Dr. Bernie S. Siegel. (New World Library; Reprint edition, 2014).

St. Teresa of Calcutta on page 54: Catholic Online. <http://www.catholic.org/clife/teresa/quotes.php>

Antoine de Saint-Exupéry on page 56: from *The Little Prince* (Harcourt Brace & Company, 1971).

Leonard Nimoy on page 63: Goodreads Quotable Quote: Leonard Nimoy <http://www.goodreads.com/quotes/131926-the-miracle-is-this---the-more-we-share-the>

A.A. Milne (from *Winnie-the-Pooh*) on page 69: from "A A Milne's Winnie The Pooh characters in quotes" in The Telegraph: Culture & Books, 14 October 2016. <http://www.telegraph.co.uk/books/what-to-read/winnie-the-pooh---aa-milnes-winnie-the-pooh-characters-in-quotes/piglet-noticed-that-even-though-he-had-a-very-small-heart-it-cou/>

Antoine de Saint-Exupéry on page 90: from *The Little Prince* (Harcourt Brace & Company, 1971).

Winston Churchill on page 106: <http://www.goodreads.com/quotes/11562-we-make-a-living-by-what-we-get-we-make>

Maya Angelou on page 107: "Great Quotes for Kids About Serving Others" by Erin DeGroff, January 30, 2016 at InspireMyKids.com <http://inspiremykids.com/2016/great-quotes-for-kids-about-serving-others/>

St. Bernadette Soubirous of Lourdes on page 119: The Catholic Reader online blog from Saturday, June 8, 2013. <http://thecatholicreader.blogspot.com/2013/06/st-bernadette-soubirous-quotes.html>

St. Teresa of Calcutta on page 120: quoted under February 9 in *Catholic Mom's Cafe: 5-Minute Retreats for Every Day of the Year* by Donna-Marie Cooper O'Boyle (Our Sunday Visitor Publishing, 2013).

About the Author

Jeanne Nealon is from a family of educators. Her father was a teacher and principal for many years, and his love for the classroom and dedication to his students inspired Jeanne to become a teacher. Her first teaching position was in 1981 at Bonita Springs Middle School. She enjoyed teaching language arts and directing the school plays. Her experiences there led to the founding of Laces of Love Charitable Foundation, Inc. with her sister, Mary Myrmo.

Jeanne has been giving spiritual and motivational talks for over 40 years. She has been the keynote speaker and presenter at many Education and Leadership Conferences. She also has been involved with many youth organizations throughout the state of Florida. Jeanne was named Teacher of the Year for Collier County Schools in 1994 and is a Golden Apple Award recipient. She recently was named one of AAUW's Women of Achievement for her contribution to the community of Southwest Florida.

After teaching middle and high school for many years, Jeanne stayed home and raised her two sons. She is an active school volunteer, a Religious Education teacher at St. William Church, and a substitute teacher when needed. She devotes much of her time to writing, speaking, and "Getting Shoes for Needy Kids." In many schools, she is known simply as "The Shoe Lady."

God is always present.
Nothing happens without His permission or outside of His will.
Anything we do to others we do to Him.
All kindness and goodness are in Him.
                    ~St. Bernadette Soubirous of Lourdes

119

Yesterday is gone. Tomorrow has not yet come.
We have only today. Let us begin.
~*St. Teresa of Calcutta*